D H Howe   T A & D L Kirkpatrick

Advance with English 2

Oxford University Press

Oxford University Press, Great Clarendon Street, Oxford OX2 6DP

OXFORD NEW YORK
ATHENS AUCKLAND BANGKOK BOGOTA BOMBAY
BUENOS AIRES CALCUTTA CAPE TOWN DAR ES SALAAM DELHI
FLORENCE HONG KONG ISTANBUL KARACHI KUALA LUMPUR
MADRAS MADRID MELBOURNE MEXICO CITY NAIROBI
PARIS SINGAPORE TAIPEI TOKYO TORONTO WARSAW

and associated companies in
BERLIN IBADAN

© Oxford University Press 1992

First published 1992
Fifth impression 1998

No unauthorized photocopying

All rights reserved. No part of this publication may be reproduced, stored in a retrieval system, or transmitted, in any form or by any means, electronic, mechanical, photocopying, recording, or otherwise, without the prior written permission of Oxford University Press.

'Oxford' is a trade mark of Oxford University Press

This book is sold subject to the condition that it shall not, by way of trade or otherwise, be lent, resold, hired out, or otherwise circulated without the publisher's prior consent in any form of binding or cover other than that in which it is published and without a similar condition including this condition being imposed on the subsequent purchaser.

Illustrated by Kathryn Blomfield, John Yeung and Gary Rees
Commissioned photographs by Victor Lam Studio
Cover: John Clementson and Raynor Design

Acknowledgements

For permission to adapt and use copyright extracts, the authors and publisher would like to thank the following:

The Hamlyn Publishing Group Ltd for *Bird Men* published in *Skyways* by R.J. Hoare.

Asia Magazine Ltd for *A Fabulous New Colour* published in *The Midnight Fox* by Betsy Byars.

The Macmillan Publishing Co Ltd for *Stop Those Hiccoughs*.

South China Morning Post for *Spidermen*.

For permission to reproduce photographs:

The Japan National Tourist Organization for the photograph of the Ginza Shopping District in Tokyo.

Oxford and District Table Tennis Association for the photograph of table tennis.

Ashley Toft and Explore Worldwide for the photograph of the Omayyed Mosque in Damascus

ISBN 0 19 426004 6

Printed in Hong Kong

Introduction

Organization of the book

This book is divided into thirteen integrated units. Each unit deals with language items and communicative functions as listed on the contents pages. For ease of reference the units are given sub headings but these should not be thought of as separate lessons: they often merely indicate the kinds of skills involved.

Comprehension

There is variety in both the content of the passages and the types of exercises. The aim is to guide the pupil to an understanding rather than simply test comprehension.

Exercises include both conventional questions and the types featured in modern examinations including cloze-type questions and both open and multiple-choice questions. The cloze-type exercises are also used as an introduction to summary writing and for consolidating new vocabulary.

Where possible, the passage and exercises that follow, occupy one double spread only to make it easier for the student to refer back to the text when answering questions.

New words

New words are printed in colour when they first appear in a passage and are usually repeated later with syllable stress markings.

Pronunciation Practice

Each unit presents at least one common pronunciation difficulty in the form of a contrast: two sounds often confused are contrasted with each other in a number of exercises.

Language Practice

The language practice ranges from simple mechanical drills to controlled sentence composition, followed later in the unit by various kinds of communicative use. All exercises should be worked orally in the first place. Exercises marked Oral need not be written out. Exercises marked Oral/Written are intended to be written out after oral practice. The written exercises are suitable for homework provided they have first been worked orally in class.

Communicative Functions

Practice of communicative functions occurs under the various headings such as Guided Conversation, Dialogues, Problem Solving, Following Instructions, Interpreting Rules and Using English. More practice is provided in the workbook.

Reading for Information

This covers: reading for exact information; reading for specific information; reading for the main idea; reading for implied meaning; note-taking; summary writing.

Spelling, Punctuation and Dictation

Spelling rules are given only where they are useful. Rules alone cannot produce good spelling. Regular exercises are given in commonly misspelt words.

Good punctuation depends on mastering the use of conventional signs and on an understanding of sentence structure. Both aspects are dealt with.

Dictation is a useful way of practising spelling, punctuation and the use in writing of new language items.

Guided Composition

The methodology in this course leads the learner gradually from exercises in which he is given a great deal of guidance, to composition which is almost entirely unguided.

Unit	Page	Comprehension	Pronunciation Practice	Language Practice
1	4	Bird Men	[-l] and [-r]	The simple past tense
2	16	Flying Saucers	[-k] and [-g]	More practice with past tense
3	28	Good Manners	[e] and [eI]	The simple present tense
4	38	A Fabulous New Colour	Revision	Preposition phrases: adverbials of time; the indirect object
5	50	The World's Greatest Inventor	[I], [e], and [æ]	*Who*, *Which*, and *Whose*; short answers and indirect questions
6	62	Spidermen	[s] and [θ]	*Many*, *much*, *a few*, *a little*, *a lot of*, *too much*, *too many*, etc.
7	74	The Lady with the Lamp	More on [e] and [eI]	*Too*; *enough*; verb pattern; *here . . .* and *there . . .* with verbs
8	86	The Road Crossing Code	–	Orders and requests; verb pattern: *make*, *let* plus *to*
9	96	The Fastest Boy in the World	[ɒ] and [əʊ]	Verb patterns with *ask*, *tell*, etc.; indirect questions with and without change in word order
10	108	Stamp-collecting	[ʌ] and [æ]	*Just*, *already*, *yet* with the present perfect tense; *still*; reflexives
11	120	Stop those hiccoughs	[ʃ] and [tʃ]	Gerunds in subject position, as direct objects and in complement position; verbs followed by *-ing*
12	132	Scouting	[tʃ] and [dʒ] [aI] and [aIə]	*What . . . for?* with gerunds; verbs, nouns and adjectives with prepositions
13	146	Making Rain	Consonant clusters	*(Not) as . . . as*; adverb clauses of reason with *because*, *as* and *since*
	158	Test Paper		
	166	Appendix 1 Spelling Rules		
	170	Appendix 2 Grammar Summary and Practice		
	174	Appendix 3 Phonetic symbols		

Guided Conversation	Using English	Reading for Information	Spelling, Punctuation, and Dictation	Guided Composition
What did you do?	–	Inventions	Past tense changes	Modern Bird Men
What happened?	Finding out about people	–	Practice with the past tense	Narrative
Habits and occupations	–	Tables	Dropping the silent *e*	Picture composition
Asking for something	Finding out about times	–	Passage for prepared dictation	Narrative
–	–	Interpreting diagrams and pictures	–	Likes and dislikes
Going camping	Talking about amounts	–	–	Picture composition
–	–	Making notes	Passage for prepared dictation	Picture composition
Permission	Expressing obligation	–	–	Instructions
Getting information	–	Reading tables; sequencing	–	A newspaper report: indirect questions
–	Describing events	–	Spelling rules	Note taking and narrative
Very polite requests and replies	–	Following written instructions	–	Letter writing
Expressing feelings	Finding out about others	–	Passage for prepared dictation	Description: position and function
Giving reasons	More comparisons	–	Punctuation: more practice with commas	Safety rules

UNIT 1

Bird Men

Most people have sometimes thought: 'I should like to fly like a bird'. Many people have tried! We do not know about all the people who have tried to fly but we know about some of them.

In about AD 1020, for example, an Englishman, Oliver, tried to fly with wings like a bird's. He covered more than two hundred metres before he crashed to the ground and broke his arms and legs. In spite of his injuries, Oliver seemed quite pleased. He said he had made one little mistake. He had forgotten to wear a tail like a bird's. But when he recovered from his injuries, he never tried to fly again.

In 1507, an Italian, named John Damian, tried to fly in Scotland. He wore a pair of wings made from hens' feathers, and leaped from the walls of Stirling Castle. He fell like a stone to the ground below, and broke a leg.

Damian was very disappointed. He said, 'I made a mistake. I used hens' feathers and hens do not often fly. I ought to have used the feathers of a bird that flies. Then I am sure I would have flown.' But when he was well again, Damian, like Oliver, never attempted another flight.

An Italian scientist, John Borelli, spent much time thinking about flying. Finally, in 1680, he wrote a book containing a great many calculations. They proved that men would never be able to fly with wings on their arms. Borelli worked out, that a man's arms were not strong enough to support him in the air.

We know now that he was right but some people took no notice of what Borelli said. In 1742, a Frenchman, although he was an old man, tried to fly across the River Seine, in Paris, with wings strapped to his arms. He leaped from the balcony of a house beside the river and went crashing down on to a boat moored at the bank of the river. He was fortunate and only broke a leg.

Today men can do much better, though they still cannot fly like birds. They use very light, strong wings called 'hang-gliders'. One man landed safely after jumping from a balloon at 11,909 metres! Another, in Hawaii, stayed in the air for nineteen hours thirty-six minutes! They still sometimes hurt themselves, however.

A Quick questions

Give short answers like these:

> Yes, he did.   No, he didn't.   Yes, they did.

1. Did Oliver try to fly?
2. Did Oliver hurt himself?
3. Did Oliver try to fly again?
4. Did John Damian try to fly in Italy?
5. Did John Damian succeed?
6. Did John Damian hurt himself?
7. Did John Borelli fly?
8. Did John Borelli write a book?
9. Did the Frenchman break his arm?
10. Did all the men who tried to fly hurt themselves?

B Think about it

Pick out the sentences that are not true and explain why they are untrue:

1. a. Oliver flew for more than two hundred metres before crashing.
   b. He broke two arms and one of his legs.
   c. When he tried to fly again he wore a tail like a bird's.
2. a. John Damian made a successful flight in Scotland.
   b. He made his wings from hens' feathers.
   c. The next time he flew he used the feathers of a bird that flew well.
3. a. John Borelli calculated that a man's arms were too weak for flying.
   b. After that no one tried to fly again.
4. a. The old Frenchman tried to fly across the River Seine.
   b. He fell into the river.
   c. He broke a leg and had other injuries.
5. Most men who tried to fly were injured.
6. Today men can fly like birds.

C *Choose the correct answer to complete these sentences.*

1 Oliver tried to fly with wings like a bird's, about... years ago.

    A 100
    B 1,000
    C 50
    D 2,000

2 John Borelli made his calculations... attempted flight.

    A before Oliver's
    B before John Damian's
    C after the old Frenchman's
    D before the old Frenchman's

New Words

Use these words to finish the sentences. You may use the words more than once.

| in 'spite of | re'covered | flight | 'finally | calcu'lations | proved |
| sup'port | took no 'notice | 'balcony | moored | 'fortunate | |

John Borelli made a large number of _____ and _____ he _____ that man could not fly like a bird because his arms were not strong enough to _____ him. _____ _____ _____ his calculations, however, men continued to try to make a successful _____ through the air. They _____ _____ _____ of Borelli's warning. A Frenchman jumped from the _____ of a house near a river and crashed down on to a boat which was _____ at the bank of the river. He was _____ and only broke his leg. He soon _____ from his injury. But _____ _____ _____ these accidents, men went on trying to fly and some were not so _____ as to escape with a broken leg or arm.

Pronunciation Practice

[-l] and [-r] after consonants

1

a clown

a crown

2

A	B	A	B
clown	crown	glow	grow
cloud	crowd	fly	fry
climb	crime	flying	frying
cloak	croak	flight	fright
glass	grass	flute	fruit
glue	grew	play	pray

3   **A**

'Everybody was 'looking at the ↘ clown
'That 'flower 'glows in the ↘ dark.

     B

'Everybody was 'looking at the ↘ crown
'That 'flower 'grows in the ↘ dark.

Language Practice

The simple past tense

This dialogue will remind you of one important difference between the simple past tense and the present perfect tense. We must use the past tense if we want to say *when* something happened. The present perfect tense is used to show that an activity is completed now. It does not tell us *when*:

> Mary: When are you going to do your homework?
> Peter: I've already done it. I did it last night.

A (Oral) *Was* and *were*

Read these questions and answers:

Q: Was it / he/she cold yesterday? last night?
Were you / they at school / the dentist / the party last Friday? on Sunday?

A: Yes, I / it/he/she was. we/they were.
Or: No, I / it/he/she wasn't. we/they weren't.

Now do this exercise in pairs. Do <u>not</u> look at your partner's part of the exercise.

S1 Ask S2 questions about his holiday. Use the words below and ask questions like those in the table above. Listen to S2's answers and tick *Yes*, *No*, etc. which are given below. Check your answers with S2 at the end.

1 ... on holiday _____ week?   Yes/No
2 _____ the weather fine?   Yes/No
3 ... at the beach often?   Yes/No
4 How often?   _____ (number of times)
5 ... at any parties?   Yes/No
6 ... good parties?   Yes/No
7 ... at any restaurants?   Yes/No
8 How many?   About _____
9 ... the food good?   Yes/No
10 ... the waiters polite?   Yes/No

S2 You wrote a letter to a friend telling him about your holiday. Part of your letter is written out below. Read it, then listen to S1's questions. Give answers like those in the tables at the beginning of the exercise. Check your answers with S1 at the end.

I was on holiday last week. It rained every day. I only went to the beach on Monday and Friday. I went to a few parties. I did not enjoy them. I went to a lot of restaurants – about fourteen. The food was delicious in all of them, but the waiters were very rude.

B (Oral) *ed* endings

Read these questions and answers:

Q:	Who	cleaned washed	the	car dishes	yesterday? last night?	A:	He/Peter They		did.

Q:	When did	he/she they	clean wash	it? them?	A:	He/She They	cleaned washed	it them	at	nine o'clock. eight forty-five.

Now do this exercise in pairs. S1's part of the exercise is below, S2's part is on page 9. Look only at your part.

S1 Imagine you are a detective. You are investigating a robbery at an office. S2 is the owner of the office. Ask S2 questions like those in the tables above using the notes below to help you. Write down S2's answers and always write the time in figures. Check your answers with S2 at the end. The first one is done as an example.

1 (arrive) ...... first at the office?
  When ....?

  S1: Who arrived first at the office?   Albert
  S2: Albert did.
  S1: When did he arrive?   9.05
  S2: He arrived at nine five.

2 (arrive) ... next at the office?
  When ...?

3 (open) ... the door?
  When ...?

4 (unlock) ... the safe?
  When ...?

5 (carry) ... the bag of banknotes out of the safe?

6 (count) ... the banknotes?
  When ...?

7 (discover) ... £10,000 was missing?

8 (telephone) ... the police?
  When ...?

S2 *Imagine you are the owner of an office. Someone has taken some money from your safe. The police have arrived. A detective, S1, is asking you questions. Study the pictures below which are in the wrong order. Listen to S1's questions and give answers like those in the tables at the beginning of the exercise. Check your answers with S1 at the end. The first one is done as an example.*

> S1: Who arrived first at the office?
> S2: Albert did.
> S1: When did he arrive?
> S2: He arrived at nine five.

C (Oral)

Answer these questions truthfully using Yes, I was No, he wasn't, Yes, we were, No, they weren't, *etc.*

1. Were you at school yesterday?
2. Were your friends at school yesterday?
3. Were you at school on Friday?
4. Were your friends at school on Friday?
5. Was it Saturday yesterday?
6. Was it Sunday yesterday?
7. Was it cold yesterday?
8. Was it hot yesterday?
9. Were you in bed last night?
10. Was it a holiday yesterday?

D (Oral)

Work in pairs. David was very busy for four days last week. The pictures below show what he did. Look at the pictures and then ask and answer questions. The first one has been done for you as an example.

| S1: Did David take an exam last week? | S2: Yes, he did. |
| S1: When did he take it? | S2: He took it on Monday morning. |

E (Oral/Written)

Look at pictures 1 and 2 and the example sentences in the box below. Then make similar sentences about the other pictures.

> Tom drew a horse...(John)   Tom drew a horse and John drew a horse, too.
> Susan did not cut her finger...(Mary)   Susan did not cut her finger but Mary cut her finger

1 Tom drew a horse...(John)

2 Susan did not cut her finger...(Mary)

3 Pat did not sweep...(Janet)

4 Mr Day drank coffee...(Mr Lee)

5 Sam did not pass...(Tony)

6 May sang a song...(Susan)

7 Tim did not swim...(Alan)

8 Mr Hill did not write...(Mrs Wit)

9 Peter ran away...(Jack)

Useful Expressions

Ago

Reply truthfully to these questions in complete sentences using *ago*. Follow the example.

> When did you see him?
> I saw him ten minutes ago. (ten minutes before now)
> When did your father begin work?
> My father began work twenty years ago. (twenty years before now)

1. When did you wake up?
2. When did this lesson begin?
3. When did you have a holiday from school?
4. When did you catch a cold?
5. When did the Headmaster speak to you?
6. When did you ride in a bus?
7. When did you do some homework?
8. When did you have something to eat?
9. When did you have your hair cut?
10. When did it rain?

Dictation

This story happened long ago in China. A ship sailed from Canton to Hong Kong. It carried a lot of money. In those days there were many robbers and they sometimes attacked ships.

One day the ship left Canton in the morning. It moved very slowly because it had a small sail and there was not much wind. The sailors on the ship were afraid. They knew that there was danger. Suddenly they saw another ship. It was small but it had a big mast and a big sail. It moved very quickly and it soon caught up with the slower ship.

The small ship was full of robbers. They climbed on to the bigger ship and attacked the sailors. The sailors fought bravely but there were more robbers than sailors. After a few minutes, the sailors stopped fighting. Some of them jumped into the sea. The robbers carried the money on to their ship and sailed away.

Guided Conversation

What did you do?

Work in pairs. Read the sample dialogue. Then make up other similar conversations. You may use words from the lists below in place of the words in boxes if you want to.

S1: 'Did you 'swim in the ↗ river yesterday?

S1: ↘ I swam in the sea , ↘ too.

S2: ↘ No, I ↘ didn't. I 'swam in the ↘ sea. 'What did ↘ you do?

1 go to the cinema	1 went to the beach
2 find ten pounds	2 found fifty pence
3 lose a pen	3 lost a pencil
4 eat two apples	4 ate five oranges
5 see a shark	5 saw a snake
6 draw a horse	6 drew a cow
7 sit at the front	7 sat at the back
8 write on the board	8 wrote in my book
9 sweep the path	9 swept the classroom
10 sing loudly	10 sang quietly

Reading for Information

Inventions

A *Study the table below.*

Inventions	Date	Inventor	Country	Definition
Aeroplane	1903	Orville and Wilbur Wright	USA	A flying machine that has an engine.
Parachute	1783	Louis Lenormand	France	Something used by people to allow them to jump from aeroplanes.
Helicopter	1907	Paul Cornu	France	A flying machine with revolving blades on top.
Airship	1900	Ferdinand von Zeppelin	Germany	A flying machine that is filled with a gas which is lighter than air and has an engine.
Glider	1853	George Cayley	England	A flying machine without an engine.
Seaplane	1911	Glenn Curtis	USA	A flying machine that can land on and take off from water.
Hot-air balloon	1783	J.M. and J.E. Montgolfier	France	A flying machine without an engine. The passengers travel in a basket that hangs below a balloon which is filled with a gas lighter than air.

Now answer these questions:

1. Who invented the helicopter?
2. When did Glenn Curtis invent the seaplane?
3. a. From which country did George Cayley come?
   b. What did George Cayley invent?
   c. When did George Cayley invent it?
4. a. Who invented the aeroplane?
   b. When did they invent it?
   c. From what country did they come?
5. a. What did Ferdinand von Zeppelin invent?
   b. When did he invent it?
6. a. Who invented the hot-air balloon?
   b. When did they invent it?
   c. From what country did they come?
7. a. Which is/are the earliest invention(s) on the list?
   b. Which is/are the latest invention(s) on the list?
8. List these inventions in the order in which they are invented: glider, parachute, seaplane, helicopter, aeroplane, airship.
9. Which inventions do not have engines?
10. Which flying machine can land on water?

B Look at these pictures of the seven inventions. Write down in your exercise book the name of each invention. The first one has been done for you.

1   A helicopter.

C Study the table below and then answer the questions on page 15.

The First Flights Across the Atlantic Ocean					
Flying machine	**Name of Captain**	**Number of crew**	**Starting point**	**Arrival point**	**Date**
Seaplane	A.C. Read	5	Canada	England	16th–17th May 1919
Bomber	J. Alcock	1 (A. Brown)	Canada	Ireland	14th–15th June 1919
English airship	G. Scott	30	Scotland	USA	2nd–6th July 1919
German airship	H. Eckener	33	Germany	USA	12th–15th October 1924
Aeroplane (*Spirit of St Louis*)	C. Lindbergh	–	USA	France	20th–21st May 1927

1 a. Who was the first person to fly single-handed across the Atlantic Ocean?
   b. In which year did he do this?
   c. From where did he leave?
   d. Where did he arrive?
   e. What was the name of his aeroplane?
2 a. How many airships are in the list?
   b. Which airship took longer to cross the Atlantic Ocean?
   c. How many people were in the German airship?
3 a. How long did A.C. Read take to fly across the Atlantic Ocean?
   b. Do you think he stayed in the air all the time? Explain your answer.
4 a. When did Alcock and Brown fly across the Atlantic Ocean?
   b. From where did they leave?
5 a. Which kind of flying machine had the most crew members?
   b. What was the Captain's name?

Guided Composition

Here is the beginning of an account of two modern 'bird men'. The first paragraph is written for you but there are some words missing. In the second paragraph, you are given verbs but you have to change them into the past tense. You are given the details for the third paragraph but you must write it yourself. Write out the whole composition.

Modern Bird Men

The 'bird men', who _____ to fly with wings made of feathers, never succeeded. They all went crashing down to earth and some of them _____ themselves. The human body is not strong _____ to fly like a bird. In modern times men have flown in aeroplanes which _____ not have engines. These _____ called gliders. They are pulled _____ the air, rather like kites. They often _____ long distances before they glide back to _____. Two men, however, _____ not want to sit in a glider. They _____ to glide wearing their own wings. Unlike the early fliers' wings, however, theirs _____ straight and strong.

Two of the most famous modern 'bird men' were Clem Sohn and Leo Valentin. They (design) their own wings. They (drop) from an aeroplane and glided down for several thousand metres. Then they (pull) the handle of their parachutes and (come) safely down to earth. They (travel) around giving displays while hundreds of people (watch). Sohn (give) his last display in France in 1937. At 3,000 metres he (jump) from his aeroplane. He (use) his wings to glide to 550 metres, and then (pull) the handle of his parachute. It (fail) to open. His second parachute also (do) not open. He (crash) to his death at 240 kilometres an hour.

Leo Valentin – parachuting teacher before becoming 'bird man'. 1948 broke world record – fell over 6 kilometres – before using parachute. Determined to make no mistakes – wings made of wood – strapped to body – could use them to control flight downward. Knew all dangers – took no chances. 22nd May 1956, Liverpool – jumped – something wrong – dived straight down – a few seconds later – dead.

UNIT 2

Flying Saucers

In 1947 the pilot of a small aeroplane saw nine strange objects in the sky over Washington in the USA. He said that they looked like saucers. Newspapers printed his story under the headline: FLYING SAUCERS.

Since then, all over the world, people have reported seeing similar strange objects. No one knows what they are or where they come from. Some people say that they do not exist, but many others say that they have seen them. Usually people on the ground have seen them but not always. Airline pilots also have reported seeing them and so have astronauts – the men who fly in spaceships.

Perhaps some people saw them only in their imagination. Perhaps some people made a mistake. But airline pilots and astronauts do not usually make mistakes of this kind. Captain Ed Mitchell, who was the sixth man to walk on the Moon, said in 1974 that he believes that some *flying saucers* are real. Many other people now believe that these strange flying objects are visiting the Earth from other worlds in space.

'They have come to look at us,' they say.

The American Government tried to find out more about these objects. It listened to a great many people who said they had seen them. But the Government committee could not decide on what the objects were. It called them UFOs, which is short for *Unidentified Flying Objects*.

Some say they have seen people in the flying saucers! In 1964, a driver of a police car in New Mexico saw a UFO landing a mile away. When he reached it, there were two small figures standing near it. They looked like little men. When he reported it on his radio, they got inside the object and flew away.

In 1973 two men were out fishing in Mississippi. They say they saw a UFO shaped like an egg. There were three creatures like men but their skins were silver in colour. They had no eyes, and their mouths were just slits. Their noses and ears were pointed. They made the fishermen get inside the UFO for a while. Then the creatures photographed them and took them back to the place where they had been fishing.

There are many other similar stories. Some are probably untrue but some may be true. No one knows.

A Quick questions

1. When did someone first see UFOs?
2. Where was he when he saw them?
3. How many did he see?
4. Why did the newspapers use the headline: FLYING SAUCERS?
5. In which country did this take place?
6. Where did the other sightings take place?
7. Where were most people who saw them?
8. Where were other people when they saw them?
9. What did the American Government do?
10. What did it set up to try to find out more?
11. What is a committee?
12. What does *unidentified* mean? (If you find this difficult, remember that you have an identity card. What does it tell people?)
13. What was the occupation of the man who saw the UFO in New Mexico?
14. What did he do when he first saw it?
15. What did he do next?
16. In which country is Mississippi?
17. What were the two men doing when they saw the UFO?
18. How many creatures did they see?
19. In how many ways were the creatures different from humans?

B Think about it

1. The writer points out that airline pilots and astronauts have seen UFOs. Why do you think he does this?
2. The writer gives the name of one person who has reported seeing a UFO: Captain Ed Mitchell. Why do you think he does this?
3. Does Captain Mitchell believe all the stories of *flying saucers*?
4. Explain, in your own words if you can, what Captain Mitchell believes.
5. Did the US Government decide that *flying saucers* do not exist?
6. What did the Government decide?
7. Which of these statements best sums up what the writer believes?
   a. All the stories are true.
   b. Some of the stories are true.
   c. Some of the stories may be true.

C Class discussion

1. Had you heard about *flying saucers* or UFOs before you read the passage? If so, what had you heard or read about them?
2. What do you think of the stories of the policeman in New Mexico and the three fishermen in Mississippi? Do you believe either or both of them?
3. Can you think of any possible explanations for some of the sightings of *flying saucers*?
4. What do you believe now?

New Words

A For each new word in list A, find its meaning in list B:

A	B
'objects	Company providing regular service of aircraft for public use.
'headline	A group of people meeting to discuss or carry out work.
ex'ist	A person who travels in a spaceship.
'airline	To be or live.
'astronaut	Things that can be seen or touched.
com'mittee	Newspaper heading in large letters.
uni'dentified	Long narrow openings.
slits	Of the same sort.
'similar	Unable to be named.

B Use the new words in the passage to complete this summary. Some past tense verbs have also been omitted.

In 1974 a pilot _____ nine strange _____ in the sky. Newspapers _____ his story under the _____ FLYING SAUCERS. Then many other people said they had seen _____ objects, though some people _____ that they do not _____. But _____ pilots and _____ in spaceships, such as Captain Ed Mitchell, said that they _____ that some flying saucers were real.

The American Government _____ up a committee to find out what the objects were but it could not. It called them _____ Flying Objects.

Some say they have seen people in the flying saucers. A policeman said that he saw two figures that _____ like little men. Two fishermen say that they _____ three creatures with silver skins, no eyes and _____ for mouths. There are many other _____ stories but no one knows if any are true.

Pronunciation Practice

[-k] and [-g]

1

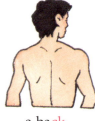
a back

a bag

a bank

a bang

2

A	B
pick	pig
lock	log
duck	dug

A	B
think	thing
sunk	sung
sinking	singing

3

A

That's a 'big ↘ lock.
He 'fell on his ↘ back.
She's 'going to ↘ sink.
She's 'stopped ↘ sinking now.
'Put it in the ↘ back.
There was a 'big 'bank near the ↘ shop.

B

That's a 'big ↘ log.
He 'fell on his ↘ bag.
She's 'going to ↘ sing.
She's 'stopped ↘ singing now.
'Put it in the ↘ bag.
There was a 'big 'bang near the ↘ shop.

Language Practice

More practice with the past tense

A These pictures show what happened to Peter yesterday. Look at the pictures and then answer the questions under each picture. Use the prompts to help you. Follow the example below.

What did Peter see yesterday?
(see a UFO)

Q: What did Peter see yesterday?
A: He saw a UFO.

1

What did he do?
(hide behind a tree)

2

What did the UFO do?
(land)

3

What happened then?
(two green men come out)

4

What did the men do?
(capture Peter)

5

Where did the green men take Peter?
(take him inside the UFO)

6

What did one of the green men do then?
(take a photograph of Peter)

7

What happened next?
(let him go)

8

What did the UFO do?
(take off)

9

What did Peter do?
(run home)

B (Oral)

Work in pairs. Take it in turns to ask and answer the questions. Follow the example.

S1: Peter/see/an aeroplane/a UFO/yesterday?
S2: saw/UFO

S1: Did Peter see an aeroplane or a UFO yesterday?
S2: He saw a UFO.

1

S1: Helen/buy/a bag/a basket/yesterday?
S2: bought/bag

2

S1: Susan/drink/coffee/tea/yesterday?
S2: drank/coffee

3

S1: John/break/a cup/a glass/yesterday?
S2: broke/a cup

4

S1: Sam/fry/a fish/an egg/last night?
S2: fried/a fish

5

S1: Edward/draw/a cat/a boat/last week?
S2: drew/a boat

6

S1: Dorothy/get/good marks/bad marks/last term?
S2: got/good marks

C (Oral)

Read this short dialogue:

> S1: Mary and Tony went to the park last Sunday.
> S2: Did they play tennis?
> S1: Yes, they did./No, they didn't.

Now work in pairs. Do <u>not</u> look at your partner's part of the exercise.

S1 It is Saturday evening. Study the diary which shows what Pat and Jim did last week. Make statements about what Pat and Jim did as in the sample dialogue above. After each statement, listen to S2's question. Using the information in the diary, answer S2's questions.

	a.m.	p.m.
Fri.	Went to the beach.	Left the beach at 5 o'clock.
Sat.		Went to the cinema. Saw an English film.
Sun.		
Mon.	Went to the airport. Met grandmother.	
Tue.		
Wed.	Went shopping. Bought two lamps.	Stayed at home. Watched television.
Thur.	Went to the post office. Posted letters.	

S2 Listen to S1's statements. After each one, ask a sensible question using words from the list below. Listen to S1's answer and put a tick or a cross beside each question in the list. The sample dialogue will help you.

> . . . leave at 3.30?   . . . see an Egyptian film?   . . . post some letters?
> . . . buy some fruit?   . . . meet their grandmother?   . . . watch television?

Guided Conversation

A Look at these nine pictures and then put them in the order in which you think they happened.

B In the story in exercise A, above, the policeman asks the boy some questions. These are written out below and on page 23. Imagine you are the boy and answer the questions using the pictures to help you. Then, in pairs, practise the conversation.

Policeman: When did you wake up?

Boy: I woke up at...

Policeman: Why did you wake up?

Boy: A bright light...

Policeman: What did you do?

Boy: I looked...

Policeman: What did you do then?
Boy: ...
Policeman: Did your mother also see the UFO?
Boy: ...
Policeman: What did she do then?
Boy: ...
Policeman: When did the UFO fly away?
Boy: ...
Policeman: What did it look like?
Boy: ...
Policeman: Were you frightened?
Boy: ...

Dictation

When the children arrived home, the Sun was sinking in the sky and it was almost dark. They ate their supper and got ready for bed. James felt very tired so he soon fell asleep. Suddenly, a loud bang shook the building. James woke up, jumped out of bed and ran to the window. He looked out of the window and saw a strange object on the pavement below. He then heard his younger brother shout, 'Something has fallen out of the sky!'

Using English

Finding out about people

Work in pairs. Do <u>not</u> look at your partner's part of the exercise.

S1 Read the dialogue below. S2 will ask you questions about it. Use the information given in the interview to answer.

An Interview with a Lecturer

Lecturer: My name is Mavis Lee. I'm thirty-eight.

Lecturer: Yes, I'm married. My husband's a dentist.

Lecturer: I teach at Cairo University.

Lecturer: Oh, I get up at about seven thirty and then I have breakfast; some toast and some coffee usually.

Lecturer: At about eight thirty. I go by car.

Lecturer: I finish at about five thirty.

Lecturer: Oh, look after our child. She's adopted. Her name's Jill. She comes from India.

She's three years old.

Interviewer: Are you married?

Interviewer: I see, and what do you do?

Interviewer: What time do you get up in the mornings?

Interviewer: And what time do you go to work?

Interviewer: What time does work finish?

Interviewer: What do you do in the evenings?

Interviewer: I see, and how old is she?

S2 Ask S1 these questions about the interview above, which he has read and note down his answers in your exercise book.

1. What is the name of the person?
2. How old is she?
3. Is she married?
4. What does her husband do?
5. What does she do?
6. What time does she get up in the mornings?
7. What does she have for breakfast?
8. What time does she go to work?
9. How does she go to work?
10. What time does she leave work?
11. What does she do in the evenings?
12. How many children has she got?
13. Where does her child come from?
14. How old is she?

S1 Now ask S2 these questions about the interview he has read, which is on page 25, and note down his answers in your exercise book.

1. What is the name of the person speaking?
2. How old is she?
3. What does she do?
4. Where does she work?
5. Is she married?
6. What does her husband do?
7. When does she get up?
8. When does she go to work?
9. How does she go to work?
10. When does she finish work?
11. Does she always cook in the evenings?
12. Does she have any children?
13. Does she often watch television?
14. What sort of books does she read?
15. When does she usually go to bed?

S2 *Now read the dialogue below. S1 will ask you questions about it. Use the information given in the interview to answer S1's questions.*

An Interview with a Doctor

Doctor: My name's Helen Smith. I'm fifty, and I'm a doctor.

Doctor: I work at the hospital.

Doctor: Yes, I am. My husband is a doctor, too.

Doctor: Oh, at about six thirty usually, and then I have breakfast.

Doctor: Well, I go to work at eight o'clock. I go by bus.

Doctor: At five o'clock usually.

Doctor: Well, sometimes I cook but sometimes my daughter cooks.

Doctor: No, I don't watch television a lot, but I read.

Doctor: Well, I usually read books about work, books about medicine.

Doctor: Usually at about eleven o'clock.

Interviewer: Where do you work?

Interviewer: Are you married?

Interviewer: I see, and what time do you get up?

Interviewer: And what time do you go to work?

Interviewer: And what time does work finish?

Interviewer: I see. What do you do in the evenings?

Interviewer: And do you watch television?

Interviewer: Oh. What sort of things do you read?

Interviewer: When do you normally go to bed?

Guided Composition

One or both of these stories may be practised orally and one chosen for written work. Tell the stories by answering the questions. You may add more things that happened.

A **A Visit to an Interesting Place.**
Where did you go?
When did you go there?
Who went with you?
What time did you leave home?
How did you go there? Did you go by bus, by car, by train or did you walk?
What time did you arrive?
What did you see first?
What did you see next?
What did you see after that?
Did anyone speak to you?
What did he or she tell you?
Did you have anything to eat or drink?
What time did you start back?
What time did you get home?
Did you enjoy the visit?
Did you find the visit interesting?

B **How I Spent a Day's Holiday.**
Where did you go?
When did you go? Was it on Thursday or Friday, or was it a special holiday?
Who went with you?
What time did you leave home?
How did you travel, by bus, by car, by train or did you walk?
What did you take with you?
What time did you arrive?
What did you do first?
What did you do next?
What did you do after that?
Did you meet anyone?
Did you have anything to eat or drink?
What time did you start back?
What time did you get home?
Do you want to do it again?

Revision Test 4

A *Read the sentences below the graph and choose the correct verb.*

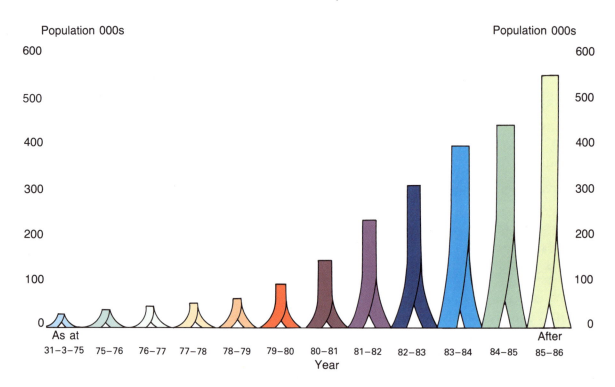

In 1975 the population of New Town (is/was/has been) only about 30,000. By 1979 it (is/had been/was still) only about 65,000, but in 1980 it (begin/is beginning/began) to rise more sharply and (has reached/reached/reaches) 150,000. The rise then (continued/was continuing/is continuing). After 1985 it (reaches/reach/will reach) about 500,000.

B *Decide which choice is the best:*

1 Someone shows you two paintings and asks you which one you like. You like each one equally well, so you reply:

  A Two.
  B Two of them.
  C Both.
  D All of them.

2 A caller on the phone asks you if he may speak to your father. You reply:

  A Wait here, please.
  B Hold it, please.
  C Just a minute, please.
  D You'll have to wait.

3 You are a stamp-collector. Someone asks you what your hobby is. You reply:

  A I collect stamps.
  B A stamp-collector.
  C I am collecting stamps.
  D Stamp-collection.

4 You arrive home to find a workman doing something to the window of your flat. You are puzzled so you ask:

  A How do you do?
  B What do you do?
  C What are you doing?
  D What is it doing?

C *For each blank, choose the best answer from the choices given.*

This is the keyboard of a typewriter. You can see (1) the letters of (2) alphabet. Altogether there are twenty-six (3) . Perhaps one day in the future you (4) to type. Many girls (5) to type so that they can work in an office and perhaps become (6) secretary. Men, too, sometimes (7) it useful to be able to type.

As long (8) as 1714, an Englishman called Henry Mill (9) a kind of typewriter but no one now (10) what it looked like or how it (11) . An American called Christopher Sholes invented something very much like the modern typewriter over a hundred years ago. The keys were arranged in (12) order; A, B, C, and so on. This (13) to be changed, however, because it was found that when the typist (14) very quickly, the letters often (15) together. This is how they dealt (16) the problem. They (17) out which letters were most often used in English. They then put (18) letters far apart on the keyboard. Then they could not be used so quickly and (19) would be less chance of them sticking. That is why the letters are in the (20) in which you see them today.

1 A all
   B every
   C both
   D some

2 A a
   B the
   C an
   D one

3 A alphabets
   B letters
   C characters
   D figures

4 A learn
   B are learning
   C have learned
   D will learn

5 A are learning
   B learn
   C will learn
   D learns

6 A the
   B a
   C an
   D for

7 A finds
   B has found
   C find
   D finding

8 A passed
   B ago
   C gone
   D now

9 A invented
   B has invented
   C is inventing
   D invents

10 A is knowing
   B are knowing
   C knows
   D knew

11 A works
   B worked
   C is working
   D has worked

12 A A,B
   B letter
   C alphabetical
   D number

13 A had
   B have
   C has
   D having

14 A types
   B is typing
   C typed
   D has typed

15 A stick
   B stuck
   C sticked
   D have stuck

16 A with
   B for
   C to
   D on

17 A find
   B found
   C founded
   D have found

18 A this
   B those
   C that
   D some

19 A the
   B it
   C they
   D there

20 A order
   B column
   C print
   D orders

UNIT 3

Good Manners

We say that a person has good manners if he or she behaves politely and is kind and helpful to others. Everyone likes a person with good manners but no one likes a person with bad manners. 'Yes,' you may say, 'but what *are* good manners? How do I know what to do and what not to do?'

Manners change as time goes by. In the picture you see Sir Walter Raleigh (*RAHlee*), a famous Englishman, who lived four hundred years ago. He is laying his cloak over a puddle of water so that Queen Elizabeth shall not get her feet wet. This pleased the Queen at the time but no one would do this nowadays. You would look silly if you did this for your teacher!

Different countries and different races have different manners. Before entering a house in some Asian countries, it is good manners to take off your shoes. In European countries, even though shoes sometimes become very muddy, this is not done. A guest in a Chinese house never finishes a drink. He leaves a little, to show that he has had enough. In a Malaysian house, too, a guest always leaves a little food. In England, a guest always finishes a drink to show that he has enjoyed it.

We must find out the customs of other races, so that they will not think us ill-mannered. But people all over the world agree that being well-mannered really means being kind and helping others, especially those older or weaker than ourselves. If you remember this, you will not go very far wrong.

Here are some examples of the things that a well-mannered person does or does not do.

He never laughs at people when they are in trouble. Instead, he tries to help them. He is always kind, never cruel, either to people or animals. When people are waiting for a bus, or in a post office, he takes his turn. He does not push to the front of the queue. If he accidentally bumps into someone, or gets in their way, he says 'Excuse me' or 'I'm sorry'.

He says 'Please' when making a request, and 'Thank you' when he receives something. He stands up when speaking to a lady or an older person, and he does not sit down until the other person is seated. He does not interrupt other people when they are talking. He does not talk too much himself. He does not talk loudly or laugh loudly in public. When eating, he does not speak with his mouth full of food. He uses a handkerchief when he sneezes or coughs.

A Quick questions

1. What word has the same meaning as *well-mannered*?
2. What happens to manners as time goes by?
3. Why did Sir Walter Raleigh lay his cloak over the puddle?
4. What was the result?
5. Where is it good manners to take off your shoes before entering a house?
6. Where would this *not* be good manners?
7. What is the meaning of the custom of not finishing a drink?
8. Why do guests in England always finish a drink?
9. What is the important thing to remember if we want to be well-mannered?
10. Where is it thought well-mannered to help others?

B Think about it

Which of these sentences do you think are true and which are untrue?

1. There is no need to know the customs of other races.
2. A person with good manners thinks of others before himself.
3. A well-mannered person is unselfish.
4. People who are in trouble often look funny and so it is not ill-mannered to laugh at them.
5. If you have paid for your seat on a bus, you should sit on the seat and not let anyone else have it.
6. If you are in a hurry, it is a good idea to push by other people.
7. Saying 'please' and 'thank you', is a waste of time.
8. A schoolboy should stand when speaking to a woman.
9. A schoolboy should not stand when speaking to a man.
10. When a person is saying something that you think is wrong, you should stop him and tell him so.

C Summary

Complete this summary by adding suitable words from the passage. Some of them will be new words, but not all:

Manners _____ as time passes. Sir Walter Raleigh's action _____ Queen Elizabeth but would look _____ nowadays. We find different manners in different _____ and _____, too, and there are many examples of this. This is why we must find out the _____ of other people so that they will not think we are _____. All over the _____, however, people agree that being well-mannered means being _____. A well-mannered person always tries to _____ other people and _____ does anything to annoy them.

D Class discussion

1. Can you think of any examples of good or bad manners not mentioned in the passage?
2. Do you think that most people in your country are well-mannered or bad-mannered?
3. Where do you think manners are learned?

New Words

Find the meaning of each of the new words.

cloak	By mistake, not done on purpose.
'puddle	Habits, ways of doing things.
'races	A small pool of muddy water.
'customs	A long loose coat without any sleeves.
ill-'mannered	A line of people waiting their turn for something.
well-'mannered	Different kinds of people.
queue	Knock against something or somebody.
acci'dentally	Polite.
bump	Asking for something.
way	Rude.
re'quest	The direction in which something or somebody goes.
inter'rupt	Stop someone who is speaking or doing something.

Pronunciation Practice

[e] and [eɪ]

1

a p**e**nny   a p**ai**nter   a d**e**bt   a d**a**te

2

A	B
g**e**t	g**a**te
w**e**t	w**ai**t
t**e**ll	t**ai**l
s**e**ll	s**ai**l
p**e**n	p**ai**n
f**e**ll	f**ai**l
l**e**d	l**ai**d
w**e**st	w**a**ste

3

A

He ′led them ↘ down.
I'm ′going to ↘ sell it.
She has a ′different ↘ pen.

B

He ′laid them ↘ down.
I'm ′going to ↘ sail it.
She has a ′different ↘ pain.

Language Practice

The simple present tense

Always, never, sometimes, often, seldom, usually, are some common adverbs of frequency. They are used to describe how often a person does something. In the list below, two of these adverbs have been given a mark. Always has been given ten out of ten to show that it is something you do ten times out of ten. Never has been given nought out of ten to show that it is something you do not ever do.

A   *Now give the other adverbs a frequency mark out of ten.*

always	10/10	sometimes	
usually		seldom	
often		never	0/10

Note: Some different answers are possible.

Notice where these adverbs of frequency occur in a sentence:

I You We They	always often usually sometimes seldom never	get up at six o'clock.

He She	always often usually sometimes seldom never	gets up at six o'clock.

B (Oral/Written)

Make six true sentences using the words in the boxes below or any other suitable words.

Every day	I we my brothers/sisters	go to	the office. school. the market. work. town.
	my brother/sister my father/mother	goes to	

C (Oral)

Read the example dialogue. Then, in pairs, ask and answer questions, like those in the example, about when you do the things listed below.

S1: What time do you get up?
S2: Do you? I get up at six forty-five.
S2: I usually get up at about six thirty.
S2: Well, I don't always get up at six thirty.

1. leave home in the morning
2. get to school
3. have lunch
4. get home in the evening
5. have supper
6. do homework
7. watch television
8. go to bed

D (Oral) *Where* and *when* with the simple present tense

1. Here is a train timetable. Below it you will see some questions and answers. Make as many more questions and answers as you can beginning When and Where. Dep. means departs or leaves. Arr. means arrives.

	Arr.	Dep.
Waterloo	–	6.45
Clapham	6.51	6.53
Woking	7.10	7.12
Basingstoke	7.45	7.47
Andover	8.10	8.12
Salisbury	8.31	8.33
Yeovil	9.31	9.33
Axminster	9.57	9.59
Honiton	10.11	10.13
Exeter	10.35	

When does it leave Waterloo?
   It leaves Waterloo at six forty-five.
Where does it go then?
   It goes to Clapham.
When does it arrive at Clapham?
   It arrives at Clapham at six fifty-one.
Where does it go then?

2   Use the train timetable in exercise 1 again. This time imagine that you have two friends who make the journey from Waterloo to Exeter once a week. Ask the same questions but this time use *What time* instead of *When*, *They* instead of *It* and *get to* instead of *arrive at*.

> What time do they leave Waterloo?
>   They leave Waterloo at six forty-five.
> Where do they go then?
>   They go to Clapham.
> What time do they get to Clapham?
>   They get to Clapham at six fifty-one.
> Where do they go then?

Reading for Information

More practice with tables

A   This table shows the postal charges for surface mail (*not* airmail) from the United Kingdom worldwide. Use the table to answer the questions below.

LETTERS PRINTED PAPERS AND SMALL PACKETS			
Weight not over	Letters (Outside Europe only)	Printed Papers*	Small Packets
20g	28p	24p	
60g	48p	35p	
100g	69p	45p	45p
250g	£1.42	90p	90p
500g	£2.70	£1.65	£1.65
1kg	£5.30	£2.95	£2.95
2kg	£10.50	£5.35	£5.35
(Max 2 kg)			

* Max wt 2 kg Except books and Pamphlets which may weigh up to 5 kg

1   How much does it cost to send a letter, weighing fifteen grams?
2   How much does it cost if the letter weighs over 100 grams but less than 250 grams?
3   How much does it cost if the letter weighs one and a half kilograms?
4   What is the heaviest weight that may be sent by post?
5   How much does it cost to send a 300 gram packet to China?
6   How much does it cost to send a letter weighing the same?
7   How much does it cost to send some books, weighing five kilograms, to Egypt?
8   How much does it cost to send a parcel, weighing two kilograms, from London to Cairo?

33

B This table shows the time taken to go from station to station on the Central line of the London Underground. It also shows how often the trains run at different times of the day. Use it to answer the questions below.

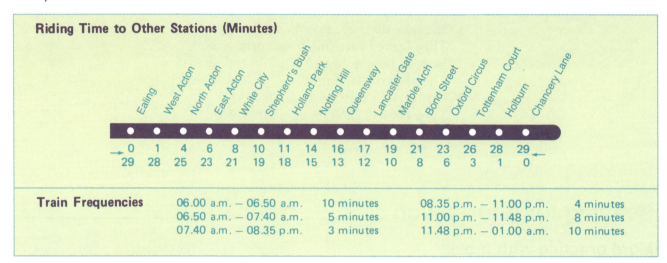

1 How long does it take to get from Ealing to Chancery Lane?
2 How long does it take to get from Chancery Lane to West Acton?
3 How long does it take to get from Shepherd's Bush to Lancaster Gate?
4 There are four journeys that take only one minute. One is Ealing to West Acton. Which are the other three?
5 Which three journeys take three minutes each?
6 At which times of the day do the trains run most frequently?
7 At which times of the day do the trains run least frequently?
8 When do no trains run?

Dialogues

Choose one of the alternatives given to complete each dialogue:

1 Tom: I never go to the cinema.
  Dick: Why not?
  Tom: ...

  A I'm always too busy.
  B They have too many films.
  C It's too exciting.
  D I don't go.

2 You say to a shop assistant. 'How much does this cost?' She replies:

  A Never mind.
  B Just a minute. I'll find out.
  C There is no price on it.
  D Please ask someone else.

Study Notes

1. We use the simple present tense of verbs for things that sometimes, often or usually happen:

    We sometimes go to the library.
    Every morning I wake up.

2. After he, she, it or a singular noun, the present simple tense uses an s in writing:

    He sometimes goes to the library.
    Every morning she wakes up.

3. For something being done *now*, we normally use the present continuous tense:

    Every day I read a newspaper.   (simple present)
    I am reading a newspaper now.   (present continuous)

Spelling

For most words that end in an e which is not pronounced (e.g. love), drop the e before a vowel but keep it before a consonant:

Here are some examples where the e is dropped before a vowel:

live + ing = living	live + ed = lived	shine + ing = shining
move + ing = moving	hope + ing = hoping	smile + ing = smiling
move + able = movable	cause + ing = causing	excite + ing = exciting

But remember these exceptions:

see   + ing = seeing   agree + ing = agreeing   agree + able = agreeable

Here are some examples where the e is not dropped before a consonant:

love + ly = lovely	move + ment = movement	use + ful = useful
wise + ly = wisely	nine + ty = ninety	

But remember these exceptions:

true + ly = truly   wise + dom = wisdom   argue + ment = argument

Guided Composition

(Oral/Written)

A *Write about these children. The first one is done for you on page 37.*

1 **John**	2 **Paula**	3 **Peter and Mary**
lives in London	lives in Oxford	live in Reading
goes to 	goes to 	go to 
gets up at	gets up at	get up at
goes to school by 	goes to school by 	go to school by 
likes English	likes Mathematics	like Geography
plays	plays	play 
does not play the	does not play the 	do not play the
in the evening listens	in the evening watches	in the evening read
goes to bed at	goes to bed at	go to bed at
is going to be a	is going to be a 	are going to be 

1. John lives in London. He goes to Holland Park School. He goes to school by bus. He likes English best. He plays football but he does not play the piano. He listens to the radio in the evening. He goes to bed at nine o'clock. He is going to be a doctor when he leaves school.

B *Now write about yourself.*

A Puzzle

Here is a very old English puzzle. If you can work out what it means, then it is true!

I C U R Y Y 4 M E

Answer: 'I see you are too wise for me.'

1 I (I) see (C) you (U) are (R) too wise (two Y's) for (4) me (ME)

UNIT 4

A Fabulous new Colour

I dreamt that I discovered a fabulous new colour, a brand-new colour that no one had ever seen before. This is what happened in my dream.

I was digging in my garden and all of a sudden, while I was just casually digging, I got a strange, exciting feeling that something exceptionally good was going to happen. I began to dig faster and faster, my heart pumping in my throat, my hands flashing in the soft black earth. Suddenly I stopped and put my hands up to my eyes because there, in the black earth, was a ball, a perfect, round ball of brand-new colour.

I was not able to believe it for a moment, because I had never seen anything but blue and green and all the usual colours, but gradually my eyes adjusted and I saw it clearly. I was the first person in the world to see this new colour.

I went into the house and said to my parents, 'I have discovered a new colour.' My parents were not particularly interested, because there is no such thing as a *new* colour, and they were expecting me to bring out a piece of paper on which I had mixed a lot of different water-colours to make an odd colour. Then slowly I took my hand from my pocket and held up the smooth, round ball of new colour.

That night I was on the news on television with my discovery and the announcer said 'Ladies and gentlemen, tonight you will see, later in our programme, a new colour, discovered today by a young boy.' By the time *I* came on the television, every person in the world was sitting in front of his set.

The announcer said, 'Now, young man, tell the world how you discovered this new colour.'

'I was outside digging in the earth.'

'Where was this earth?'

'Just in my garden. Then I had a strange feeling.'

'What was this strange feeling like?'

'It was the feeling that I was about to make a new and important discovery.'

'I see. Go on.'

I dug deeper and deeper, and then I looked down into the earth and I saw *this*!' I showed the new colour, and all around the world a silence occurred. The only silence that had ever fallen upon the whole world at one time. Eskimos paused with pieces of dried fish halfway to their mouths; Russians who had run in from the cold stopped beating the snow from their arms; fishermen left their nets. Then, together, all at once, everyone in the world murmured, 'Ahhhhhh.'

A Quick questions

You need not always answer in complete sentences. Use your own words as far as possible.

1 What did the writer discover in his dream?
2 Where was he digging?
3 Why did he begin to dig faster and faster?
4 Why did he stop digging?
5 What did his discovery look like?
6 Who did he tell first about his discovery?
7 Did his parents believe him at first?
8 What did they think he would show them?
9 What did he actually show them?
10 What television programme did he go on?
11 How many people watched the programme?
12 What happened when he showed his new colour on television?
13 What did the Eskimos stop doing when they saw the new colour?
14 Why did everyone say 'Ahhhhhh'?

B Think about it

1 Did the writer know he was going to discover something when he began digging?
2 Do you think the writer painted a lot? Why? Why not?
3 What does *this* in line 34 refer to?
4 What time of year do you think it was?
5 Why did fishermen stop looking after their nets?
6 Did the writer really discover a 'fabulous new colour'?
7 What would you like to discover?

New Words

Use these new words to complete the sentences:

| 'casually | dis'covered | 'suddenly | a'djusted | brand-new |
| ex'ceptionally | pumped | 'gradually | 'murmuring | |

1. The scientist, Harvey, _____ that the heart _____ blood around the body.
2. When I first walked into the dark cinema, I could not see anything. My eyes, however, _____ _____ to the dark and I could see better.
3. In the middle of his speech, Richard heard some people whispering and _____, so he waited until they stopped.
4. Martin did _____ well in his exams, so his parents bought him a _____ calculator.
5. The policeman approached the thief _____ in order not to be noticed. He then _____ grabbed him and arrested him.

Pronunciation Practice

Revision

1

a seat

a sheet

a hut

a heart

a pill

a pail

a cloud

a crowd

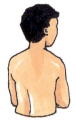

Tom's back

Tom's bag

locks

logs

2 a.

A	B
see	she
cut	cart
kick	cake
glass	grass
peck	peg
locks	logs
so	show
duck	dark
fill	fail

b.

A	B
pleasant	present
duck	dug
seats	seeds
sip	ship
much	march
hit	hate
cloud	crowd
sink	sing
nips	nibs

Language Practice

Preposition phrases: adverbials of time; *have breakfast*, *have a lesson*, etc.

A (Oral)

Read this passage and then answer the questions beginning with the words given:

Peter gets up at nine o'clock on Fridays but on Saturdays and the other school-days, he gets up at seven fifteen. He has a bath at seven thirty and has breakfast at seven forty-five. He usually has soup, bread and a cup of tea. Sometimes he has jam on his bread and on Fridays he has an egg. He goes to school at eight o'clock and he has his first lesson at half past eight.

In the morning break he has something to drink and sometimes, if he has any money, he has some sweets. He has lunch at one o'clock and sometimes he has a game of football with the other boys. He has his first lesson of the afternoon at two fifteen and he goes home at four twenty. On Tuesdays and Wednesdays he has a piano lesson. He has his supper at eight o'clock and he goes to bed at ten thirty.

1. What time does Peter get up on Fridays? On Fridays he . . .
2. What time does he get up on Saturdays and the other school-days? On . . .
3. What does he do at seven thirty? He . . .
4. What does he usually have for breakfast? For breakfast he usually . . .
5. What does he sometimes have? He . . .
6. What is different about breakfast on Fridays? He . . .
7. What time does he go to school and what time does he have his first lesson?
8. What does he do in the morning break?
9. When does he have lunch?
10. What does he sometimes do in the lunch break?
11. When does he have his first lesson of the afternoon?
12. When does he go home?
13. What happens on Tuesdays and Wednesdays?
14. When does he have his supper and when does he go to bed?

B Asking for information

Read the sentences below:

When What time	do you	get up go to bed	on	Tuesdays? Thursdays? Fridays?
What		have for lunch		
How many times a week		eat ice-cream?		

I	usually always	get up go to bed	at	eight thirty ten o'clock	on	Tuesdays. Thursdays. Fridays.
		have noodles	for	lunch		
		eat ice-cream		three times a week.		

Work in pairs to complete the questionnaire below. S1 asks S2 the questions and writes down S2's answers. The tables above will help you. When the questionnaire has been filled in with all S2's answers, change over, so that S2 asks the questions and writes down S1's answers.

Questionnaire

These questions were answered by (name) _____ on _____.

1. time/get up/Mondays? _____
2. time/get up/Fridays? _____
3. time/go to bed/Tuesdays? _____
4. time/go to bed/Saturdays? _____
5. time/finish homework/Wednesdays? _____
6. have for breakfast/Saturdays? _____
7. have for dinner/Fridays? _____
8. times a week/have a Physical Education lesson? _____
9. nights a week/watch television? _____
10. times a week/buy sweets? _____

Now use the information in the questionnaire to write down eleven sentences about your partner. Begin like this:

My class-mate is called _____. On Mondays he/she gets up . . .

C (Oral/Written)

Mr Lee is 80 years old. The table below shows what Mr Lee does (Action); how often he does these things (Frequency) and what time he does these things (Time). Study the table and make ten sentences to describe what Mr Lee does. The first one is done for you.

> Mr Lee always goes for a walk on Sunday mornings.

What Mr Lee does		
Frequency	Action	Time
always	go for a walk	on Friday mornings
often	do exercises	in the mornings
usually	have a rest	in the afternoons
never	go to bed	after 10 p.m.
sometimes	visit his friend	on Saturdays
always	read the newspaper	before breakfast
usually	have breakfast	at 7 a.m.
never	watch television	in the evenings
always	get up	at 5.30 a.m.
usually	have a bath	at the end of the day

Making and responding to requests; the indirect object

D (Oral)

Read these questions and answers. Then do the exercise on page 44.

Q:				
Can you	lend	me	ten pounds?	
	bring	her	some food?	
	write		a letter?	

A:									
Yes, I can	lend	you	ten pounds.				lend	you	five.
	bring	her	some food.	Or:	No, but I can		bring	her	a drink.
	write	him	a letter.				write	him	a card.

Now do this exercise in pairs. Do <u>not</u> look at your partner's part of the exercise.

S1 Look at the pictures below and make a request to S2 for each one. The questions in the table on page 43 will help you. Tick S2's answers, either Yes or No, beside each picture. If the answer is No, make a brief note of what S2 can do for you. Check your answers with S2 at the end. The first one is done as an example.

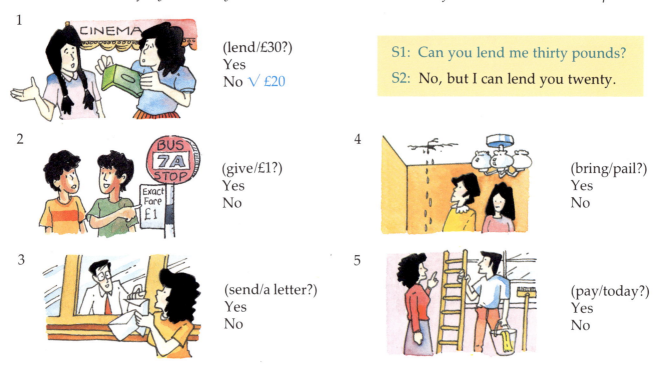

1. (lend/£30?) Yes / No ✓ £20

   S1: Can you lend me thirty pounds?
   S2: No, but I can lend you twenty.

2. (give/£1?) Yes / No

3. (send/a letter?) Yes / No

4. (bring/pail?) Yes / No

5. (pay/today?) Yes / No

S2 Listen to S1's questions. Look at the pictures below and decide which one the question is about. Using the prompt words given, reply to S1's questions with sentences like those in the table at the beginning of this exercise. The first one is done as an example.

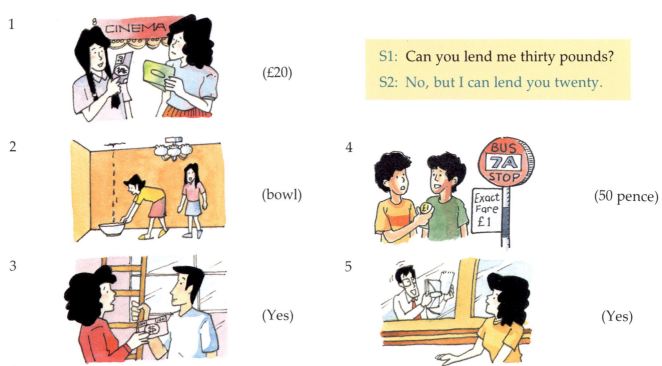

1. (£20)

   S1: Can you lend me thirty pounds?
   S2: No, but I can lend you twenty.

2. (bowl)

3. (Yes)

4. (50 pence)

5. (Yes)

E (Oral)

Work in pairs to make up a dialogue using the prompts below. Do <u>not</u> look at your partner's part of the exercise.

S1 Start the dialogue by saying to S2, either sentence a., b., or c., below. Then listen to S2's response. Continue the dialogue by choosing a., b., or c., each time. Choose sensible responses.

S1: a. I'm hungry. Will you cook me a meal?
    b. I'm thirsty. . . . bring me a drink?
    c. I'm bored. . . . read me a story?

S2: . . .

S1: a. Could you get me a coke?
    b. . . . boil me an egg?
    c. . . . read me a detective story?

S2: . . .

S1: a. Which book do you mean?
    b. There are some in the fridge.
    c. I've only got ten pounds.

S2: . . .

S1: a. You can keep the change.
    b. Here you are.
    c. They were bought yesterday.

S2: . . .

S2 Listen to S1 who will start the dialogue. Then respond each time by choosing an appropriate sentence a., b., or c.

S1: . . .

S2: What would you like me to a. cook for you?
                                b. get for you?
                                c. read to you?

S1: . . .

S2: Yes, if you a. give me one.
               b. give me the money.
             c. give me the book.

S1: . . .

S2: a. The one with the red cover.
    b. That's more than enough.
    c. Are they fresh?

S1: . . .

S2: a. Then they should be good.
    b. Thanks very much.
    c. Where shall I start?

Using English

Finding out about times

A Mrs Tripp wants to fly to Bangkok in Thailand on Tuesday. She phones a travel agent in order to find out about the times of planes. Read the dialogue and then answer the questions on page 47.

Travel Agent: Good morning, Skylark Travel.

Mrs Tripp: Good morning. Could you give me some information about planes to Bangkok, please?

Travel Agent: Certainly, when do you want to travel?

Mrs Tripp: On Tuesday, please.

Travel Agent: I see. Do you want to fly in the morning or in the afternoon?

Mrs Tripp: In the morning.

Travel Agent: There are three planes on Tuesday morning. They leave at 0815, at 0930 and at 1145.

Mrs Tripp: When does the 0815 plane arrive in Bangkok?

Travel Agent: It arrives in Bangkok at 0430 on Wednesday.

Mrs Tripp: Fine. Could you book me on that plane, please?

Travel Agent: Certainly. Could you give me your name, please?

1 To which city does Mrs Tripp want to fly?
2 When does she want to fly?
3 Why is she phoning the travel agent?
4 What is the name of the travel agent's company?
5 Does she want to fly in the morning or in the afternoon?
6 How many planes are there on Tuesday morning? What time do they leave?
7 When does the 0815 plane arrive in Bangkok?
8 How long does the journey take?
9 Which plane does Mrs Tripp want a ticket for?
10 What exactly does she say?

B   (Oral)

Work in pairs. S1 is a travel agent who works for 'Skylark Travel'. S2 is a customer who wants to fly to Beirut on Wednesday. Below is a timetable of flights to Beirut. S2 phones 'Skylark Travel' and S1 uses the timetable to answer his questions. Complete the conversation using the dialogue in exercise A as a guide.

S1: Good morning, Skylark Travel.

S2: Good . . . Beirut, please?

S1: Certainly, . . .

S2: On Wednesday, please.

S1: I see. Do you want . . . ?

S2: In the afternoon.

S1: There are . . . on Wednesday afternoon. They leave . . .

S2: When does the 1500 plane arrive in Beirut?

S1: It arrives . . .

S2: Fine. Could . . . ?

S1: Certainly. Could . . . ?

CAIRO – BEIRUT TIMETABLE

Day	Depart Cairo	Arrive Beirut
Wednesday	0745	0910
	1100	1225
	1330	1455
	1500	1625
	1700	2025

Guided Conversation

Asking for something; agreeing and refusing

We often use Could you, when asking for something, especially when we are not sure that the other person has what we want. Even if we are sure, it is always polite to begin with Could you:

'Could you 'lend me a ↗ ruler, please?

Notice the rising intonation in the example above. This is a question. We do not know whether the other person has what we want, or whether they are willing to lend it to us, so our request is in the form of a question. An order would be quite different.

'Give me 'that ↘ ruler!

Practise this conversation around the class. Use your own words in place of pencil, thumb-tacks, etc. The person spoken to may agree or refuse:

John: Could you | give me / lend me / let me have | a pencil, / some drawing-pins, / sugar, | please?

Betty: Yes, of course. Here you are. Will this one/these/this/do?
      Or:
I'm sorry. I haven't got one/any.

John: Thanks. That/Those will be fine?
      Or:
Never mind. I'll ask someone else.

Dictation

I dreamt that I discovered a new colour one day. I was digging in my garden. I got a strange feeling that something exciting was going to happen. I dug deeper and deeper. Suddenly I saw a perfect, round ball in the earth. It was a brand-new colour.

I took it to my parents. They were very interested. But they did not really expect a new colour. Later I was on the news on television. The announcer asked me to show my new discovery. Everyone in the world saw it. Everyone murmured, 'Ahhhhhh'.

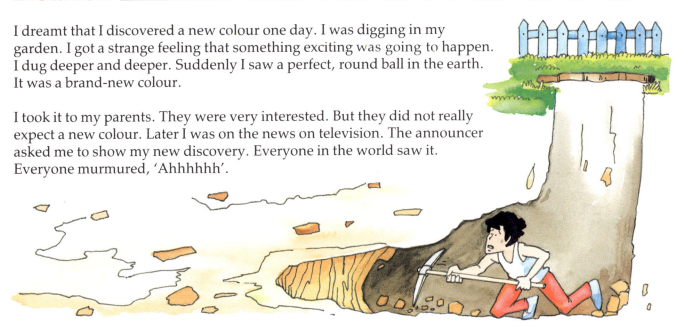

Guided Composition

A (Oral/Written)

Write an account of how you spent yesterday. If yesterday was a holiday write about last Thursday. Some questions are given below to help you to decide what to say. Be careful with tenses. Most of the time you will be using the past tense but sometimes you will use the simple present tense. The questions will help you as far as midday. You must write the rest without help.

1. What time did you wake up?
2. Do you usually wake up at that time?
3. What time did you get up?
4. Did you have a shower?
5. Did you wash your hands and face?
6. Did you comb your hair?
7. Did you brush your teeth?
8. What time did you have breakfast?
9. Where did you have breakfast?
10. What did you have for breakfast?
11. What time did you leave home?
12. What time did you get to school?
13. What time did you have your first lesson?
14. What other lessons did you have before break?
15. Did the teachers explain anything to you?
16. Did the teachers read anything to you?
17. Did the teachers give you any homework?
18. What time did you have a break?
19. Did you have anything to eat or drink?
20. What lessons did you have after the break?
21. What lessons do you have every day?
22. Where did you have lunch?
23. What did you have for lunch?
24. What happened then?
25. What time did you go home?

B *In the composition above you wrote about the kind of things that happen almost every day. Now write about some of the different things that you do on different days. Begin with Saturday.*

> On Saturday we have games in the afternoon.
> On Saturday evenings I usually . . .

49

UNIT 5

The World's Greatest Inventor

The hundreds of inventions made by Thomas Edison include the electric light bulb, the world's first 'talking machine' – the record-player, and the film-projector. Even when he was a very young boy, he was always trying to find out how things worked. In the conversation below, his father, Sam Edison, is talking about him to a friend, Captain Bradley.

'He is always asking about things,' said Sam Edison. He was proud of his son and pleased to get the chance to talk about him. 'I expect he's gone up to the farm to bother the people there with his questions.'

'The other week he went to the grain store, and climbed to the top, to watch the grain pouring in. He leant over too far and fell in. If one of the men hadn't seen him and pulled him out, he'd have been killed.'

The Captain laughed.

'Then there was the time he wanted to know how a bees' nest in the hedge worked. He looked in and nothing happened, so he began prodding with a stick. Just then a goat came and pushed him into that bees' nest, and the bees didn't like it a bit. You should have seen his face and hands when he came rushing home!'

'That lad will go a long way,' Captain Bradley said. 'It's good for him to find out things, as long as he does no harm.'

'He never does any harm – except to himself and his clothes.' As he finished speaking, Sam Edison wrinkled up his nose and sniffed. 'Can you smell something burning?' he asked, getting to his feet.

'There's smoke over there,' the Captain said, and the two men went into the street.

'It seems to come from the direction of the farm. Why, there's my son, running as if there were a wild animal after him.'

The 'wild animal' was a very angry farmer!

'Set my farm on fire, would you?' he was roaring.

Sam Edison went into the house and then came out again with a very long stick.

'Why did you do it?' he asked in a terrible voice.

'I wanted to see what would happen,' answered his son.

'Come with me, and I'll show you.' Sam Edison took him by the hand and led him down the street.

That is how the world's greatest inventor was publicly caned at the age of six in the market place of Milan, Ohio, in the year 1853.

A Quick questions

Some of the answers are begun for you:

1. How many inventions were made by Thomas Edison?
2. When did he first take an interest in how things worked? When...
3. Who invented the electric light bulb, the record-player and the film-projector?
4. Why did he fall into the grain store? He...
5. Why did he prod the bees' nest? To...
6. Why did he fall into the bees' nest? A...
7. What did the bees do? They...
8. What did Sam Edison smell? He...
9. What did the captain see?
10. What was Thomas Edison doing when they saw him? He...
11. Who was the 'wild animal' after him? It...
12. What had Edison done?
13. Why had he done it?
14. What happened as a result?

B Think about it

1. Why was Sam Edison pleased to have a chance of talking about his son?
2. Why do you think he was proud of him?
3. Why did the boy go to the farm?
4. How would he have been killed if he had not been pulled out of the grain store?
5. Sam Edison said, 'You should have seen his face and hands', after Thomas fell into the bees' nest. What did he mean?
6. Captain Bradley said, 'That lad will go a long way.' What did he mean?
7. After setting the farm on fire, Thomas said that he did it to see what would happen. What do you think he meant?
8. Sam Edison said that he would show Thomas what happened. What did he mean?

C Put a suitable word in each blank space. Some of the words, but not all, will be found in the passage:

Even when he was still a small boy, Thomas Edison, the famous _____, was always trying to find out more about how things _____. For example, he once fell into a grain _____ and was nearly killed. There was another _____ when he prodded a bees' nest to see what would _____. A goat pushed him into the nest and he was badly _____. His father was usually _____ with the boy's wish to know about things and thought that he would do _____ in life. One day, however, Thomas went _____ far. He set a farm _____ fire to see what would happen. What happened was that his father _____ him in the market place for _____ to see.

New Words

Use these new words to finish the sentences below and on page 53. You may change the form of the word, e.g., prod – prodded, wrinkle – wrinkles.

in'clude	bulb	pro'jector	'bother	grain	hatch
'publicly	hedge	prod	'wrinkle	sniff	

1. He thought that the snake was dead but when he _____ it with a stick, it moved.
2. The old woman's face was covered with _____ but she looked happy and healthy.
3. 'Don't _____ me,' she said. 'Please go away.'
4. The teacher brought a _____ into the classroom to show the children some films.

5 'Don't _____,' said the teacher. 'Please use your handkerchief.'
6 The small hard seeds of plants like wheat and rice are known as _____.
7 In England the countryside is divided up into fields with _____ around them.
8 Some plants have a round part which is planted under the ground. Roots grow down from it and leaves grow up from it. This is called a _____ and other things with the same shape have the same name. We have electric light _____ and sometimes in science lessons we use glass tubes with a _____ at one end.
9 In the old days murderers used to be put to death _____ and many people went to watch.
10 When you pack the picnic basket, don't forget to _____ something to drink.

Pronunciation Practice

[ɪ], [e] and [æ]

1

a pin   a pen   a pan

2

A	B	C
tin	ten	tan
bit	bet	bat
pit	pet	pat
sit	set	sat
lid	led	lad
big	beg	bag

3

A
'This 'pin is ↘ useless.
'Would you 'like a ↗ bit?
They 'sit the exami ↘ nation.
'What a 'big ↘ pit!

B
'This 'pen is ↘ useless.
'Would you 'like a ↗ bet?
They 'set the exami ↘ nation.
'What a 'big ↘ pet!

4 *Read aloud:*

a. The 'beggar had a 'big 'bag 'full of ↘ money.
b. 'Pat' sold the 'tin for 'ten 'thousand ↘ dollars.
c. She 'asked them to 'sit ↘ down and 'when they had 'sat ↘ down, she 'set 'cups, 'saucers and 'plates on the ↘ table.

Language Practice

Who, Which and Whose: short answers and indirect questions

A (Oral)

Practise questions and answers about the illustrations like these:

> Q: Who bought some oranges?   A: Mary did.

> Q: Which boy has a yellow shirt?   A: Jack has.
> Q: Which girls have brown shoes?   A: Mary and Susan have.

B (Oral)

Work in pairs. Look at the picture above. S1 asks questions beginning, Who or Which about each one. S2 answers. Follow the examples.

> Q: Do you know who bought some oranges?   A: Yes, I do. Mary did.
> Q: Do you know which girls have brown shoes?   A: Yes, I do. Mary and Susan have.

C (Oral)

Work in pairs. S1 makes questions beginning with Whose. S2 gives short answers. First, read the example below.

> S1: Whose pencil is broken?   S2: John's is.

S1 Do *not* look at S2's part of the exercise. Look at the pictures below. Ask a question about each picture as in the example above. Follow the correct order, 1 to 9. Listen to S2's answer and write the name he gives under the appropriate picture. The first one is done for you.

1. ruler/broken — Marian
2. bicycle/old
3. cat/black
4. window/broken
5. book/torn
6. bicycle/new
7. cat/white
8. basket/full
9. garden/pretty

> S1: Whose ruler is broken?
> S2: Marian's is.

S2 Do *not* look at S1's part of the exercise. Write the numbers from 1 to 9 in any order, beside the names in the box below. Then listen to S1's questions. Reply as in the example, giving the name from the box which is beside the number of the question he asks. The first one is done for you.

> S1: Whose ruler is broken?   S2: Marian's is.

_____ Mr Lee	_____ Helen	_____ Mr Taylor	_____ Mrs Wilson
_____ Jack	_____ Mary	__1__ Marian	_____ Mr Green

D (Oral)

Work in pairs with the same partner you had for exercise C to check that S1 wrote the correct names under the correct pictures. First, read the example below. Then S2 asks a question about each picture in exercise C and S1 replies giving the name he/she wrote under the picture.

> S2: Do you know whose ruler is broken?   S1: Yes, I do. It's Marian's.

E (Oral)

Read these sentences:

Q:	Do you know who	lost	the wallet?
		came	first in the race?

A:	No, but I know who	found	it.	It was	Judy.
		came	last.		Alan.

Now do this exercise in pairs. S1 must <u>not</u> look at S2's part of the exercise on page 57 and S2 must <u>not</u> look at S1's part of the exercise.

S1 *Look at the pictures and prompt words below. Ask a question about each one as in the table above. Remember to use the past tense. Listen to S2's reply and write what he says. Check your answers with S2 at the end. The first one is done for you.*

1

S1: Do you know who broke the chair?
S2: No, but I know who repaired it. It was Jack.
    Jack repaired it.

break/chair

2 write/board　　3 cook/fish　　4 arrive/first　　5 be/present

6 lend/money　　7 pass/exam　　8 ask/question　　9 open/window

56

S2 Look at the names in the box below. Choose one name for each action listed below and write it in the blank space. Listen to S1's questions and make replies as in the example table at the beginning of the exercise using the information in the list. The first one is done for you.

| Lily | Simon | Jack | Ann | Daisy | Ken | Jim | Jane |

1 Jack repaired the chair.
2 _____ ate the fish.
3 _____ was absent.
4 _____ failed the exam.
5 _____ cleaned the board.
6 _____ arrived last.
7 _____ borrowed the money.
8 _____ answered the question.
9 _____ opened the window.

> S1: Do you know who broke the chair?
> S2: No, but I know who repaired it. It was Jack.

F (Oral/Written)

If you know the answers to these questions, give them in a short form. If you do not know or if you are not sure, say so in complete sentences. For example, if you were asked: 'Which is the highest mountain in the world?' *you could reply:*

> Mount Everest is.
> *Or:* I'm not sure which is the highest mountain in the world but I think Mount Everest is.
> *Or:* I don't know which is the highest mountain in the world.

1 Which is the highest building in New York?
2 Which is the most crowded district in Cairo?
3 Which is the biggest reservoir in Egypt?
4 Which is the oldest monument in Egypt?
5 Which is the biggest land animal in the world?
6 Which is the biggest sea creature in the world?
7 Which is the biggest city in England?
8 Which animal is the largest that ever lived?
9 Which bird is the biggest in the world?
10 Which four-footed animal can run faster than any other animal?
11 Which animal lives the longest?

G (Oral)

Read the questions and answers below then do the exercise on page 58.

Q:

Who will	lend	me	a	ruler?
				pen?
	get			drink?

A:

I will	lend you	mine.
Mary will		hers.
I will	get you one.	

57

Now do this exercise in pairs. Do <u>not</u> look at your partner's part of the exercise.

S1 Look at the pictures below. Ask S2 questions like those in the table at the bottom of page 57. Write the name S2 says under the appropriate picture and check them together at the end. The first one is done for you.

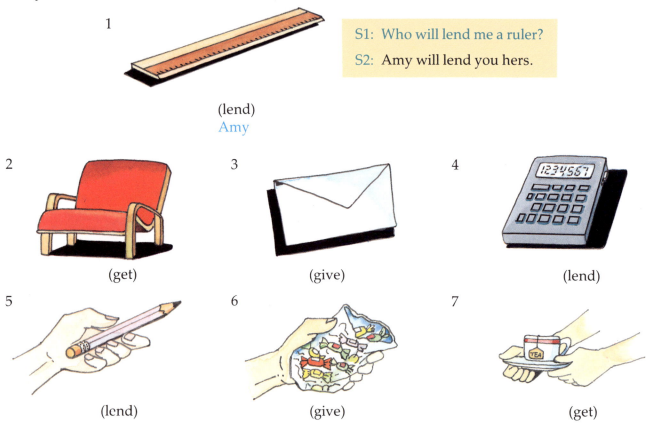

S2 Look at the pictures and prompt words below and on page 59. Listen to S1's questions. Reply using any name you choose, or with 'I', as in the example table at the beginning of this exercise. Write the name you choose (or 'I') under the picture. Check your answers with S1 at the end. The first one is done for you.

5
(mine)

6
(his)

7
(one)

Study Notes

1 In Units 4 and 5 we have practised using verbs that have an object and an indirect object. Often we may use to or for, or we may change the word order:

Q:

	Subject	Verb	Indirect object	Object
Can	you	write	him	a letter?

	Subject	Verb	Object	Indirect object
Can	you	write	a letter	to him?

A:

	Subject	Verb	Indirect object	Object
Yes,	I	can write	him	a letter.

	Subject	Verb	Object	Indirect object
Yes,	I	can write	a letter	to him.

2 We may use pronouns like mine and one in place of the direct object in the same pattern:

Who will lend me a ruler?   I will lend you one.
Who will give me a rubber?   Betty will give you hers.

3 We also practised using verbs that cannot be followed by the indirect object without to:

I can lend you £30. I can give thirty pounds to you.

Reading for Information

Interpreting diagrams and pictures

A Work in pairs. Below are ten pictures which show you, step by step, how to make a kite. Study the pictures and then read the instructions which are in the wrong order. Match them with the pictures. Now write out the instructions in the correct order. The first two are done for you.

> 1 Take two sticks of bamboo. One stick must be longer than the other.
> 2 Tie the two sticks together to form a cross.

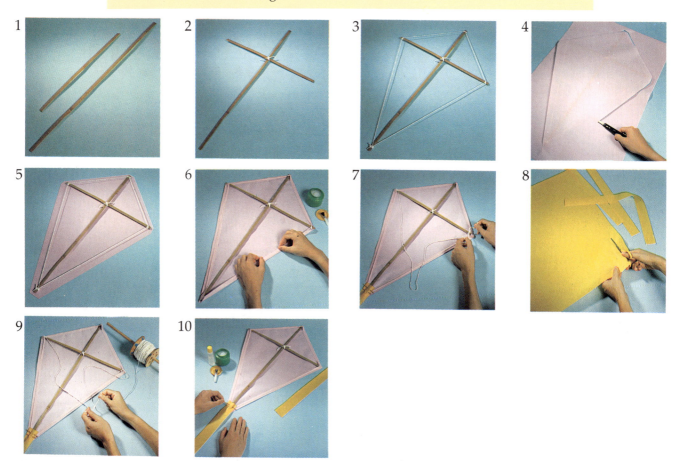

Instructions

a. Tie the two sticks together to form a cross.
b. Cut out a piece of strong thin paper. The paper must be a little larger than the frame.
c. Take a piece of string. Tie this piece of string to the ends of the shorter stick of bamboo.
d. Join the ends of the sticks with a piece of string to form a frame.
e. Pin the tail on to the bottom of the kite.
f. Cut some strips of paper to make a tail.
g. Finally, take a ball of string. Tie it to the string which is tied to the short stick of bamboo.
h. Place the frame onto the cut-out piece of paper.
i. Take two sticks of bamboo. One stick must be longer than the other.
j. Fold the edges of the cut-out paper over the pieces of string which make the frame and stick them down.

B *In this unit you read about the inventor, Thomas Edison. One of his inventions was the electric light bulb. Below is a diagram of a modern light bulb. Study the diagram and then answer the questions.*

An electric light bulb

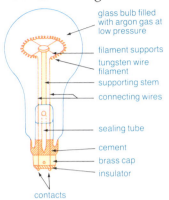

1. What is the bulb made of?
2. What is the bulb filled with?
3. What do the connecting wires connect?
4. What is the wire filament made of?
5. What is the cap made of?
6. How many filament supports are there?

C *Now study the diagram again and then complete this description of an electric light bulb.*

The bulb is made of _____ and is filled with _____. Inside the bulb there is a _____ that is supported by four filament supports. The wire filament is made of _____. It is connected to the contacts by _____. The supporting stem holds up the _____, the four _____ and the two connecting _____. The light bulb _____ is made of _____. Above the cap there is some _____. Below the cap there is an _____.

Guided Composition

A (Oral/Written) Likes and dislikes

1 *Complete these sentences about some of your likes and dislikes. In the first sentence, say what you like or dislike and in the second sentence, say why you like or dislike it.*

a. The day of the week I like most, is _____.
   On ...
b. The day of the week I like least, is _____.
   On ...
c. The month of the year I like most, is _____.
   In ...
d. The month of the year I like least, is _____.
   In ...
e. The part of the day I like most, is ...
   In/At ...
f. The part of the day I like least, is ... In/At ...
g. The school subject I like most, is _____. I like it because ...
h. The school subject I like least, is _____. I dislike it because ...

B *Work in pairs. Ask your partner how he completed the sentences above. Ask questions and give answers like these:*

> Q: Which day of the week do you like most/least?
> A: Fridays
> Q: Why do you like Fridays most/least?
> A: Because ...

Now use this information to write a short composition. Write about three likes and three dislikes of your own and three likes and three dislikes of your partner. Begin like this:

The day of the week I like most is _____. On ... The day of the week my friend, (name), likes most is _____. On ... he/she ...

UNIT 6

SPIDERMEN

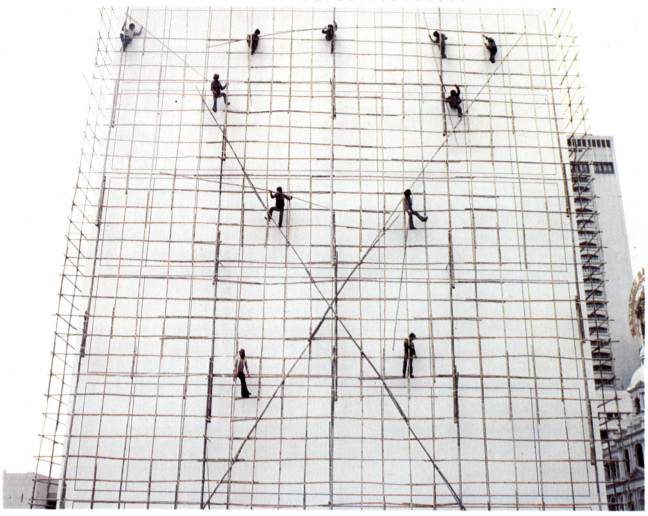

Visitors to the Far East are always amazed by the sight of 'spidermen' – the men who weave huge webs of bamboo scaffolding around buildings under construction. Of course men do similar work in the West. Whenever a building is constructed, scaffolding is necessary for the men working on the outside of the building. In the West, however, the scaffolding consists of strong metal tubes, fastened together with metal bolts. In the Far East, the scaffolding is made of bamboo.

The visitor sees buildings covered in a web of bamboo, which does not look very strong. The bamboo itself is tied together with thin strips of nylon string, which look even weaker. He sees men climbing swiftly and confidently all over this weak-looking structure, like spiders weaving a web, and he can hardly believe his eyes.

'What happens when there is a storm?' he asks.

The answer is usually, 'Nothing'! In storm after storm, bamboo scaffolding has proved itself to be as good as, or better than, metal. In 1964 there were two 25-storey buildings under construction in Hong Kong. One had bamboo scaffolding, the other had metal. The typhoon tore away the metal scaffolding and badly damaged the building. The bamboo bent and swayed with the wind, but did not break.

For thousands of years, bamboo has been trusted for its strength and its ability to sway and bend with the wind without breaking. Every day the scaffolding builders of the Far East trust it with their lives.

A Quick questions

Your answers need not be in sentences. Sometimes one word is enough.

1. Who is surprised when they see the scaffolding builders of the Far East?
2. What does a weaver usually make?
3. What insect weaves a web?
4. Who uses the scaffolding?
5. What is scaffolding made of in the Western countries?
6. How is it joined together?
7. What is a bolt? A kind of...
8. What is scaffolding made of in the Far East?
9. With what is it tied together?
10. Why do the strips of nylon string not look very strong?
11. Does the story about the 1964 typhoon show that bamboo scaffolding is weaker or stronger than metal scaffolding?
12. Why can bamboo scaffolding withstand storms?

B Think about it

1. Explain why visitors are amazed when they see bamboo scaffolding.
2. Why are the scaffolding builders sometimes called 'spidermen'?
3. With what is their bamboo scaffolding compared?
4. What does the visitor think will happen in a storm?
5. To what does the word *it* refer in the last line of the passage?

C A cloze passage

The passage below continues the article about the 'spidermen' of Hong Kong but some words have been omitted. Fill in each blank with a suitable word. In each case use only one word.

The main supports are huge poles about twelve metres high with a diameter at the bottom of about twenty centimetres. The bottoms of these are simply placed _____ the ground. They carry huge grids of bamboo made up of narrower poles. These poles are usually about 8 cm thick. Each square in the grid _____ about 75 cm by 75 cm. They are small _____ for the scaffolding builders and the construction workers _____ climb from one to another. Short bamboo poles about a metre _____ are used to fasten the whole framework to the outside _____ the building.

The scaffolding builders work quickly. Often a complete building is clothed in scaffolding in a couple of days. Good _____ can put _____ or take down _____ 65 square metres in a day! Skilled scaffolding builders are paid well, and the women who work with them are _____ well, too. These women help by passing up the bamboo poles _____ be tied on to the grids. When scaffolding is being taken _____, the women also skilfully catch the poles as they are thrown down to them, perhaps _____ a height _____ ten metres or more!

New Words

Use these new words to finish the sentences.

| weave | 'scaffolding | con'struction | bolts |
| 'confidently | 'trusted | a'bility | sway |

1 To _____ usually means to make cloth by crossing threads under and over each other. We also say that spiders _____ webs. The writer thought that the _____ around buildings under _____ in the Far East looked like spiders' webs.
2 A screw is used for joining pieces of wood together, but for fastening metal parts, _____ are used. These usually have threads on one end, on to which a nut is threaded.
3 I watched the man climb up the ladder to the top diving-board in the swimming-pool. He walked _____ to the end of the board because he _____ in his own _____.

Pronunciation Practice

[s] and [θ]

1

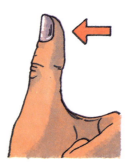

a sum   a thumb   He's sinking.   He's thinking.

2

A	B
sin	thin
sink	think
sick	thick
sing	thing
sank	thank
'some | thumb |

3

A
'That's a 'sick ↘ dog.
There's 'something 'wrong with 'this ↘ sum
He's 'going to ↘ sink

B
'That's a 'thick ↘ dog.
There's 'something 'wrong with 'this ↘ thumb
He's 'going to ↘ think

Language Practice

***Much, Many**, a few, a little,* **a lot of** with countable and uncountable nouns

A (Oral/Written)

Use the table to make sentences about the flowers and the water in the drawing:

There	is	a lot of not much a little	water	in the	vase. glass.
	are	a lot of not many a few	flowers	on the	table.

B (Oral) Questions and answers about quantity

Read the questions and answers below.

> S1: How much ink is there in the cupboard?
> S2: There is a lot of ink in the cupboard.
>
> S1: How many pens are there in the cupboard?
> S2: There are only a few pens in the cupboard.
>
> S1: How much chalk is there in the cupboard?
> S2: There is only a little chalk in the cupboard.

Now work in pairs. S1 must not look at S2's part of the exercise which is on page 66 and S2 must not read S1's part of the exercise.

S1 *Look at the list of items below. Ask questions like those in the examples above, to find out how much or how many of each item S2 has in the cupboard. Write down S2's answers and check them together at the end. The first one is done for you.*

> S1: How much bread is there in the cupboard?

1	bread	a little	5	sugar	_____
2	oranges	_____	6	grapes	_____
3	milk	_____	7	tea	_____
4	apples	_____	8	nuts	_____

S2 *Look at the items on the shelves below. Listen to S1's questions and give answers like those at the beginning of the exercise. S1 will write down your answers. Check them together at the end. The first one is done for you.*

> **S2:** There is only a little bread on the shelves.

C (Oral) Too much, too many, too few, too little, not enough

Read these sentences. Then do the exercise on page 67.

There	are	too	many few	people players	in the	lift. team.
		not	enough			
	is	too	much little	tea water		cup. glass.
		not	enough			

66

Work in pairs. Do <u>not</u> look at your partner's part of the exercise.

S1 Look at the pictures. Make a statement, like those in the table on page 66, about each picture using the word given in the box below. Some of the statements will be true and some of them will be false. S2 will listen to each statement and write down T or F for each one. Check S2's answers at the end. The first one is done for you.

1   S1: There are too many people in the car.

1	many	5	not enough	9	little
2	much	6	much	10	many
3	few	7	few	11	much
4	little	8	much	12	few

1 people 2 ink 3 plates 4 ice
5 people 6 meat 7 matches 8 fruit
9 bread 10 cushions 11 milk 12 blankets

S2 Write the numbers 1 to 12 in your exercise book. Then look at the pictures above. Listen very carefully to S1's statement about each picture. Decide whether each one is True or False and write 'T' or 'F' beside the number of the picture. Check your answer with S1 at the end. The first one is done for you: 1 T

D (Oral) *A small/large amount of*

Read these questions. Note: Who's = Who has.

> Who's got a large/small amount of money in the bank?
> Who's got a large/small number of coins in her purse?

Work in pairs. Do <u>not</u> look at your partner's part of the exercise.

S1 Look at the pictures. Ask S2 a question about each one like the example questions above. In your exercise book, write down S2's answers and check them with S2 at the end. The first one is done for you.

1
> S1: Who's got a large amount of money in the bank?
> S2: Eric.   *Or:* Eric has.

S2 Listen to S1's questions. Give answers using the words below. S1 will write down your answers; check them together at the end.

cakes – Alice	money – Eric
rice – Amy	books – Tom
coins – Peter	plants – David
nuts – Alan	hair – Bob

68

Guided Conversation

Going camping

Two people are going camping but they are going with different groups. In this conversation, they are checking to see if they have enough supplies. Work in pairs to complete the conversation by choosing one of the alternatives (a., b., c., etc) each time. S1 covers S2's part of the exercise and S2 covers S1's part of the exercise.

S1 *Start the conversation by asking S2 the question below.*

S1: Have you got enough
    a. cups?
    b. tea?
    c. rice?
    d. plates?

S2: ...

S1: How a. many / b. much more do you need?

S2: ...

S1: That's too a. many, / b. much, I can only give you a. two. / b. one kilo.

S2: ...

S1: Sorry, I can't. I've only got a small a. amount / b. number for myself.

S2: ...

S2 *Listen to S1's first question. Make a response using one of the alternatives listed. Then continue the conversation. Choose a sensible response, from the choices given, each time.*

S1: ...

S2: No, I've only got a
    a. a little.
    b. a few.
    c. a small amount.
    d. a small number.

S1: ...

S2: I'd like another a. six. / b. three kilos.

S1: ...

S2: Can't you let me have a. a little more? / b. a few more?

S1: ...

S2: All right. I'll buy some more tomorrow.

Using English

Talking about amounts

A *Mrs Tripp has just returned from Bangkok. She is going through Customs at the airport. Read the dialogue and then answer the questions.*

Customs Officer: Excuse me, madam, have you anything to declare?

Mrs Tripp: To declare?

Customs Officer: Yes. Have you got any cigarettes or perfume, for example?

Mrs Tripp: I haven't got any cigarettes, but I do have some perfume.

Customs Officer: How much have you got?

Mrs Tripp: Oh, only four bottles.

Customs Officer: Four bottles? But you're only allowed to have one bottle. I'm afraid you'll have to pay tax on the others.

Mrs Tripp: Oh, dear.

Customs Officer: What else have you got in your suitcase?

Mrs Tripp: I've got some rather interesting jewellery.

Customs Officer: How much have you got?

Mrs Tripp: Oh, half a dozen ruby rings and two beautiful jade necklaces.

Customs Officer: I see. You'll probably have to pay tax on those as well.

Mrs Tripp: Really, how much?

Customs Officer: We'll work that out later. Have you got anything else?

Mrs Tripp: I have some cigars for my husband.

Customs Officer: How many?

Mrs Tripp: A hundred.

Customs Officer: Oh, dear. I'm afraid you're only allowed to have fifty. I'm afraid you'll have to pay tax on the other fifty. Is that everything?

Mrs Tripp: Yes, it is.

Customs Officer: Well, if you'd like to go with my colleague, he'll work out how much you'll have to pay.

1 Where is Mrs Tripp?
2 Who is she speaking to?
3 Has she got any cigarettes?
4 How much perfume has she got?
5 How much jewellery has she got?
6 How many cigars has she got?
7 How many items will she have to pay tax on?

B (Oral)

Work in pairs. S1 has just returned from Manila and is going through Customs. S2 is a Customs Officer. Use the information in the table and, using the dialogue in exercise A as a guide, complete the conversation below.

Item	How much/many S1 has	How much/many allowed
Perfume Cigarettes Cigars	5 bottles 300 cigarettes 75 cigars	1 bottle of perfume 100 cigarettes *Or* 50 cigars

S2: Have you anything to declare?

S1: Yes, I have. I have _____ perfume.

S2: How _____ perfume have you got?

S1: ...

S2: You'll have to pay tax on _____ bottles. Have you anything else?

S1: Yes, I ... cigarettes.

S2: How ... got?

S1: ...

S2: Three hundred? You'll have have to pay tax on two hundred. Have you got _____ cigars?

S1: Yes, I have.

S2: How ... got?

S1: ...

S2: Well, I'm afraid you'll have to pay tax on all of them.

C (Oral)

Work in pairs. Do <u>not</u> look at your partner's part of the exercise. Different countries allow different amounts of certain items to be brought into the country without paying tax. Make up questions and answers like those in the examples below, about the amounts allowed in the countries in your part of the exercise.

> Q: How many bottles of perfume is a person allowed to take into Malaysia without paying tax?
> A: One bottle.
>
> Q: How much perfume is a person allowed to take into New Zealand without paying tax?
> A: One hundred grams.

S1 Study the table below. Ask S2 how much or how many of the items listed, a person is allowed to take into New Zealand and Thailand. Use the information in the table to answer S2's questions.

Country	Cigarettes		Cigars	Perfume
Malaysia	200	Or	50	1 bottle
Japan	400	Or	50	1 bottle

S2 *Study the table below. Use the information in it to answer S1's questions. Then ask S1 how much or how many of the items listed, a person is allowed to take into Malaysia and Japan.*

Country	Cigarettes		Cigars	Perfume
New Zealand	200	Or	50	1 bottle
Thailand	200	Or	250 grams	1 bottle

Revision Test 1

For each blank space choose the best answer from the choices given below.

It is generally __(1)__ that we are gradually __(2)__ our planet and ourselves. To be __(3)__ we __(4)__ clean air, water and food.

Unfortunately our air is not clean __(5)__ we are polluting __(6)__ with poisonous gases from factories, power stations and cars. We are burning more and more fossil fuels __(7)__ as oil and coal. This is __(8)__ more and more carbon dioxide into the atmosphere which in turn is causing a global __(9)__ in temperature.

We are producing gases which are destroying the ozone layer __(10)__ the earth. This is allowing __(11)__ harmful radiation to __(12)__ the earth and cause more skin cancers.

Our water is not clean because we are poisoning our rivers and oceans with __(13)__ and minerals __(14)__ kill fish and mammals. Deadly chemicals in the air are producing acid rain which kills trees and __(15)__ our drinking water. The effect on the food we eat can __(16)__ be guessed.

1. agreeable
   agree
   agreed ✓
   agreeing

2. disturbing
   destroying ✓
   deciding
   describing

3. health
   healthy ✓
   healed
   hopeful

4. *need* ✓
   needing
   needed
   are needing

5. while
   reason
   because ✓
   during

6. them
   us
   him
   it ✓

7. *such* ✓
   example
   as
   such as

8. planning
   putting ✓
   performing
   production

9. risen
   rising
   rise ✓
   rose

10. next to ✓
    above
    near
    under

11. *many* ✗
    any
    more
    less

12. arrive
    land ✗
    beam
    reach

13. chemistry
    chemicals
    chemist ✓
    chemical

14. *which* ✓
    who
    what
    when

15. *polluting* ✗
    pollution
    pollutes
    pollute

16. easy
    easily ✓
    early
    ease

72

Guided Composition

Use the pictures and questions below to write a story called 'An Accident'. Begin like this:

Yesterday afternoon, Peter walked home from school. He . . .

At which house did he stop?
What was there round it?
What were some men doing? (climb/scaffolding)
What did Peter buy from a hawker?
Then what did he do? (watch/men working)
Suddenly, what did one of the men do?
What did he land in? (pile)
What did the men's friends do?

When did the ambulance arrive?
Where did it take the man?
Then who came?
What did they do? (ask everyone)
What did Peter tell them about? (accident)
What did they write down?
Then where did Peter go?
What did he tell his parents about?

73

UNIT 7

The Lady with the Lamp

When Florence Nightingale was a young girl, in the early part of the nineteenth century, hospitals were not as good as they are now, and nurses were sometimes very careless and ignorant. The doctors, especially the army doctors, did not know enough about healing wounds and curing diseases. A great many of the poor soldiers in the Crimean* War died of wounds and fever because the doctors were not skilful enough to cure them.

When Miss Nightingale was a little girl, she used to like playing with her dolls and pretending to nurse them. She used to visit the poor people near her house and look after them when they were ill. She wanted very much to be a nurse, but her father said, 'Look at the women who do nursing nowadays! I don't want you to be like that!' He had plenty of money and let Florence travel to many other countries. He hoped she would forget about wanting to be a nurse.

But Florence did not forget. Wherever she went, she visited hospitals and convents where nuns were trained to be nurses. She worked in them herself and learned all she could because she was very sad to hear about the poor English soldiers dying in the crowded hospitals. Then she was placed in charge of a small hospital in London.

She wrote to some very important people and at last one of her friends, who was the Minister of War, allowed her to go and look after the wounded soldiers. She picked the best nurses she could find and took them with her. They found the hospital crowded and dirty. There was not enough medicine. There were not enough bandages. There was not even enough food. Miss Nightingale and her nurses had to work very hard indeed.

Miss Nightingale herself worked harder than anybody. She worked all day to see that the wounded soldiers were well looked after and properly nursed. Every night she walked around the hospital with a small lamp, visiting the patients. The soldiers were very pleased to see her. They knew that she was working very hard for them and they gave her the name of 'The Lady with the Lamp'. She and her nurses saved hundreds of lives and she stayed at the hospital until the war was over.

She fell ill herself because she had worked too hard for a very long time. When she came back to England, however, she started to train nurses in all the hospitals. Soon all the big hospitals in England had their own training-schools for nurses. Hospitals became clean and cheerful places and nurses were much more skilful. Today, nurses all over the world remember 'The Lady with the Lamp'.

*pronounced 'cry-ME-an'

A Quick questions

1. Are hospitals today better or worse than in Florence Nightingale's time?
2. We are told that the nurses were *ignorant*. What does this mean?
3. Who else was ignorant?
4. Why did many soldiers die?
5. What game did Florence Nightingale play with her dolls?
6. When did she look after the poor people near her house?
7. A convent is a place where nuns live. What kind of convents did Florence visit?
8. Why did she work in them herself?
9. Why did she want to learn about nursing?
10. Where was the hospital she was first put in charge of?
11. Who allowed her to go and look after the wounded soldiers?
12. Whom did she take with her?
13. We are told that there were five things wrong with the hospital she went to. What were they?
14. Who worked hardest in the hospital?
15. What did she carry when she visited the soldiers at night?
16. What did they call her?
17. How long did she stay at the hospital?
18. Why did she become ill?
19. What did she do when she returned to England?
20. What happened as a result?

B Think about it

1 Which of the endings makes a sentence that is not true?
   When Florence was a little girl...
   A she became a nurse.
   B she visited poor people when they were ill.
   C she wanted to be a nurse.
   D she pretended to be a nurse.

2 We are told that Florence Nightingale's father did not want her to become a nurse because he...
   A was afraid she would catch a disease.
   B wanted her to make a lot of money.
   C did not want her to be like the other nurses.
   D did not want her to leave home.

3 When Florence Nightingale was a young girl...
   A hospitals were managed well.
   B nurses were always careless and ignorant.
   C doctors knew less than they know today.
   D only a few wounded soldiers died.

4 When she arrived at the hospital in the Crimea, she found that there was a lot of...
   A medicine.
   B food.
   C dirt.
   D space.

C Class discussion

Which of these, in your opinion, do we need most: nurses, bus-drivers, teachers, lawyers or policemen?

New Words

Use these words to finish the sentences. You may change the form of the words and you may use them more than once.

| 'ignorant | heal | wher'ever | 'convent | nurse |
| train | in charge of | pick | 'patients | |

1 The chief nurse of a hospital is called the Matron. She is _____ _____ _____ all the other nurses.
2 The soldier had a bad wound which took a long time to _____.
3 The person in charge of a Government department in many countries is called a Minister. For example, the person _____ _____ _____ the Army, the Navy and the Air Force is usually the Minister of Defence.
4 She went to a college to be _____ as a teacher.
5 When he was ill, he stayed at home at first and his wife looked after him. Then he became worse and had to go to hospital where they could _____ him properly.
6 'I know nothing about it,' he said, 'I am completely _____.
7 He visited many countries and _____ he went, he made lots of friends.
8 She could not decide which dress to buy but in the end she _____ a red and white one.
9 Nuns live in a _____.
10 Sick people who are looked after by doctors or nurses are called _____.

Pronunciation Practice

[e] and [eɪ]

1

a p**e**n

a p**ai**nter

a d**e**bt

a d**a**te

p**e**pper

p**a**per

2 a.

A	B
let	late
wet	wait
get	gate
led	laid

b.

A	B
tell	tail
sell	sail
fell	fail
pen	pain

c.

A	B
west	waste
chest	chased
rest	raced
letter	later

3 *Read aloud. The letters printed in red are pronounced* [eɪ]

The g**a**me was being pl**ay**ed in the usual pl**a**ce. The pl**ay**ers were about equal in **a**ge and w**ei**ght and no one had managed to br**ea**k through and pl**a**ce the ball in the net. Again and again they tried but they always f**ai**led.

Then one of the pl**ay**ers on the school side (I forget his n**a**me) was kicked in the leg. The other pl**ay**ers went to his **ai**d because it was pl**ai**n that he was in gr**ea**t p**ai**n. He br**a**vely went on pl**ay**ing but he was l**a**me. Just before the end of the g**a**me the other team almost scored. The l**a**me pl**ay**er managed to get in the w**ay** of the ball and s**a**ved the g**a**me.

77

Language Practice

A (Oral)

Read these questions and answers:

Q: | Why didn't you | answer | the | question? |
| | eat | | oranges? |

A: | Because | it | was | | difficult | | answer. |
| | | too | | | to | |
| | they | were | | sour | | eat. |

Now do this exercise in pairs. Do not look at your partner's part of the exercise.

S1 Look at the prompt words below. Ask S2 questions, like those in the table above, using the prompt words. Listen to S2's answers and write them down briefly in your exercise book. Check what you have written with S2 at the end. The first one is done for you.

> 1 ... eat the meat?
> S1: Why didn't you eat the meat?   S2: Because it was too tough to eat.
> (Write '1 tough' in your exercise book.)

2 ... drink the tea?   6 ... climb the hill?
3 ... lift the weights?   7 ... jump over the fence?
4 ... wear the black shoes?   8 ... get into the taxi?
5 ... buy the camera?   9 ... buy the belt?

S2 Look at the words below. Listen to S1's questions. Give answers, like those in the table at the top of this page, using one word from the box in each answer. There are more words than you need. Number the words you use in your answers. Check the words S1 has written down at the end. The first one is done for you.

> S1: Why didn't you eat the meat?   S2: Because it was too tough to eat.
> (Write the number 1 beside 'tough' in the box below.)

_____ tight	_____ steep	_____ crowded	_____ heavy
_____ light	__1__ tough	_____ hot	_____ deep
_____ warm	_____ difficult	_____ sweet	_____ expensive

B (Oral/Written)

Read these sentences:

> 1 The meat was too tough to eat.
> 2 The shoes were too tight to wear.

Now make four sentences like number 1 above and four sentences like number 2 above.

Enough

C (Oral)

Read these questions and answers:

Q: Why couldn't | he | reach | the | shelf?
                | they | carry | | piano?

A: He wasn't tall enough.
   They weren't strong enough.

Now do this exercise in pairs. Do <u>not</u> look at your partner's part of the exercise.

S1 Look at the prompt words below. Ask S2 questions, like those in the table above, using these prompt words. Write S2's answers briefly and check them with S2 at the end. The first one is done for you as an example.

1. she/carry/case
   S1: Why couldn't she carry the case?   S2: She wasn't strong enough.
   (Write: '1 strong' in your exercise book.)

2. he/go to/school
3. he/run in/races
4. she/go to/office
5. they/play/basketball
6. you/answer/question
7. he/join/police force
8. she/drink all/water
9. they/buy/house

S2 Look at the words in the box below. Listen to S1's questions. Give answers, like those in the table at the beginning of exercise C, using one word from the box in each answer. There are more words than you need. Number the words you choose. Check them with S1 at the end. The first one is done for you.

S1: Why couldn't she carry the case?   S2: She wasn't strong enough.
(Write the number 1 beside 'strong' in the box below.)

___ clever	___ fast	_1_ strong	___ thirsty
___ old	___ big	___ well	___ tall
___ slow	___ rich	___ hungry	___ lucky

79

D (Oral/Written)

Read these situations and then answer the questions.

1. James saw a nice pair of shoes in a shop window. He went into the shop to buy them. Unfortunately the shoes cost £20 and James only had £10.

   a. What did James see?
   b. Where did he see them?
   c. Why did he go into the shop?
   d. How much were the shoes?
   e. How much (money) did James have?
   f. Make up a sentence about the shoes, using too expensive.
   g. Make up a sentence about James, using enough.

2. Last Sunday it was very windy so Monica and Mary went to the playground with their new kite. When they arrived, the wind stopped and the air became very still. Although they tried for half an hour, they could not get their kite to stay in the air.

   a. Where did Monica and Mary go?
   b. Why did they go there?
   c. What happened to the wind when they got there?
   d. How long did they try and fly their kite?
   e. Make up a sentence about the air, using too still.
   f. Make up a sentence about the wind, using enough.

Verb patterns: *here*... and *there*... with the verbs *be*, *come* and *go*

E (Oral)

Read the questions and answers below. Then do the exercise on page 81.

Have you got my pen?	Yes, here it is.
Will you lend me your books?	Yes, here they are.
Can you see my brother?	Yes, there he is.
Can you see the boats?	Yes, there they are.
Is the bus coming?	Yes, here it comes.
Are the girls coming?	Yes, here they come.
Is the train leaving?	Yes, there it goes.
Are the boats leaving the harbour?	Yes, there they go.

Now do this exercise in pairs. Do <u>not</u> look at your partner's part of the exercise.

S1 Look at the pictures and prompt words below. Ask S2 questions, like those on page 80, using the prompt words. Listen to S2's answers, and write what he says, either 'here' or 'there' for each picture. Check your answers with S2 at the end. The first one is done for you as an example.

S2 Look at the pictures below. Listen to S1's questions. Decide which picture each question is about and number it. Give answers like those in the table at the beginning of exercise E. Check S1's answers at the end. The first one is done as an example.

Reading for Information

The Alexandrian Genius

About two thousand three hundred years ago, the most famous inventor of his time was born. His name was Ctesibius (pronounced te-SEE-beeus) and he was the son of a poor barber in Alexandria.

Ctesibius was both a practical engineer and a theoretical physicist. He first showed his inventive mind in his father's barbers shop when he invented a mirror which could be adjusted to any position. The mirror was held in place by a lead ball which moved inside a tube under air pressure.

All his life Ctesibius was interested in pneumatics, the science of the mechanical properties of gases. He wrote about and taught the subject.

Alexandrian engineers were very fond of devising ingenious mechanical toys. They made statues which moved and mechanical birds which sang. Ctesibius' most famous trick was a drinking horn which produced a musical note when water was poured out of it.

Ctesibius was the inventor of the water organ. Modern organs are powered by air and the latest ones are electronic. The water organ was powered by water pressure. During Roman times it became very popular and was the favourite instrument of the emperor, Nero.

The Alexandrian's other inventions included an air-powered catapult, a water clock and a pump. His clock was far more accurate than earlier types because the outflow was precisely controlled by taps. This water clock operated all kinds of mechanical effects such as ringing bells, moving puppets and singing birds.

In Ctesibius' day, the poor people of Alexandria lived in crowded blocks of flats which were sometimes five storeys high. Because the buildings were made of wood, there was always a terrible danger from fire. Ctesibius invented a pump which probably saved thousands of lives in Alexandria and later in other cities. The pump had pistons worked by a rocker-arm which pivoted on a post in the centre. It could pump both air and water but it was used mainly for fire-fighting. It became the normal equipment of Alexandrian and then Roman fire brigades.

1. When and where did Ctesibius live?
2. Was he from a rich family?
3. Was he a purely theoretical engineer?
4. How did he first demonstrate his inventions?
5. Which science interested Ctesibius the most and what did that science cover?
6. What did the Alexandrian engineers often do to impress the public? Were these inventions useful?
7. Which of Ctesibius' inventions were mainly for amusement?
8. Which of his inventions had a practical use? What were the uses?
9. Describe Ctesibius' most useful invention and why it was so valuable to so many people.
10. Would Ctesibius' skills be of any use today? Why?

Making notes

A Read this passage about Florence Nightingale and study the notes in the box.

Florence Nightingale was born in Florence, a city in Italy, in 1820. She was named after the city.

In 1853, she went to Paris to study nursing. In the same year she went to London and established a hospital for sick women.

In 1854, she went to the Crimea where she nursed many of the wounded soldiers. She returned to London after the Crimean War in 1856.

In 1857, she established the *Nightingale Home* for the training of nurses and between 1862 and 1890, she helped establish many other nursing schools.

When she was eighty-seven she received the Order of Merit from the King of England. She died in 1910 in London, at the age of ninety.

Date	Event
1820	Born in Florence, Italy, therefore named Florence.
1853	a. Studied nursing in Paris. b. Established hospital for women in London.
1854–1856	Nursed soldiers during Crimean War.
1856	Returned to London.
1857	Established *Nightingale Home*.
1862–1890	Established other nursing schools.
1907	Received Order of Merit (aged 87).
1910	Died in London (aged 90).

B Read the passage about Margaret Thatcher. Then copy out the notes in the box and complete them.

Margaret Roberts was born on 13th of October 1925 in a town called Grantham in England.

In 1951, at the age of twenty-six, she married Dennis Thatcher. Two years after her marriage she became a lawyer and then, in 1959, she became a politician. She became Prime Minister of England in 1979. In 1983 she was re-elected Prime Minister. She resigned in November 1990.

Date	Event
1925	?
?	Married Dennis Thatcher.
?	Became a lawyer.
1959	?
1979	?
?	Re-elected Prime Minister.
1990	Resigned

C *Read the passage about Helen Keller. Then copy out the notes and complete them.*

Helen Keller was born on the 27th of June 1880 in Alabama in the United States. When she was only two years old she became very ill and, although she did not die, she became deaf, dumb, and blind. After a great deal of hard work and effort she managed to speak her first sentence when she was ten years old. The sentence was, 'It is warm'. After that she made so much progress that in 1896 she was able to go to college. She graduated with honours four years later.

In 1936, her dearest friend and teacher, Anne Sullivan, died. Ten years later she suffered another tragedy when a fire destroyed her home and many of her valuables.

In 1955, the American nation honoured her on her seventy-fifth birthday. She died in 1968 at the age of eighty-eight.

During her life she wrote several books. These books include: *The Story of My Life*, which she wrote in 1902; *The World I Live In*, which she wrote in 1910; and *Helen Keller's Journal*, which was published in 1938.

Date	Event
1880	?
?	Became deaf, dumb and blind.
1890	?
1896	?
?	Graduated from college (with honours).
1902	?
?	Wrote *The World I Live In*.
1936	?
1938	?
?	House and valuables destroyed by fire.
1955	?
1968	?

D *Read the passage and then make your own notes about the life of Marie Curie.*

Marie Sklocowska was born in Poland on the 7th of November 1867. In 1891 she moved to Paris. There she met Pierre Curie and married him in 1895. She was a brilliant scientist and in 1903 she won the Nobel Prize for Physics because she had discovered radioactivity.

In 1906 she became Professor of Physics at the University of Paris. She was the first woman to become a Professor at that University. In 1911 she won another Nobel Prize, this time for Chemistry!

In 1921 she moved to the United States. She died in 1934 at the age of seventy-seven.

Dictation

Florence worked harder than anybody. She made sure the wounded soldiers were well looked after and properly nursed. Every night she walked around the hospital with a small lamp, visiting patients. They were pleased to see her and called her, 'The lady with the lamp'. She and her nurses saved hundreds of lives.

Guided Composition

(Oral/Written)

1 Work in pairs. Look at the picture story below about Denis. Take turns to ask and answer questions about the pictures. The phrases in the box will help you.

reading	night-time	happened	bulb	postcard
reach	too high	stood	still too high	nurses
stool	fell	hurt	hospital	

2 Now write your own composition saying what happened to Denis. Begin like this: *One night last week, Denis was reading. Suddenly the light went out. He went . . .*

3 Look at the last picture in exercise 1. Denis wrote a postcard to his friend Jill. He told her what was wrong with him. He told her what happened and when he expected to go home. Imagine you are Denis. Write Denis's postcard to Jill. Do not write more than five sentences.

UNIT 8

The Road Crossing Code

Some years ago all children used to learn something called *Kerb Drill*. (Kerb means the edge of the pavement.) This was a set of rules for crossing a busy road safely. Then the rules were improved and new rules were made. These are called the *Road Crossing Code*. (Code here means a set of rules.) The Government published a pamphlet to help parents to teach the *Road Crossing Code* to their children.

Even if you are not a parent, you should know the Code, and you should be able to teach it to younger children, if necessary, and to see that they obey it. This is what the pamphlet says. (Some of the words have been changed a little.)

Why change the Kerb Drill?

The increase in speed and volume of traffic, and the fact that many children learnt the *Kerb Drill* by heart without knowing its full meaning, have led to the new *Road Crossing Code* being produced. It is the result of a lot of research. It is suitable for school children, but not for children who are too young to go to school. They should not be allowed on the road alone.

Will you please help your children to learn the meaning of the Code and how to use it?

Do not forget that your child's road safety is your responsibility. Setting a good example, whether walking or driving, is at all times essential

The meaning of the Road Crossing Code

1 First find a safe place to cross, then stop. Safe places to cross, which should be pointed out to children, are:

Bridges

Subways

Pedestrian crossings (or zebra crossings as they are sometimes called because of the black and white stripes)

Where a policeman, a school crossing patrol or a school road safety patrol is controlling the traffic

Where there are none of these, the child must be shown how to find a safe place. This means a place where there are no parked cars and there is maximum visibility in both directions. For example, there may be a crossing place marked with metal studs. This may, or may not, have a safety island in the middle of the road.

Remember to tell your child that he, or she, does not have the right of way on crossing places marked with studs and must use them with great caution.

When the child has found a safe place to cross, he must stop and...

2 Stand on the pavement near the kerb.
He should choose a place where car drivers can see him and he can see approaching traffic. He should stand slightly back from the edge of the road. Now he is ready to...

3 Look all round for traffic and listen.

4 If traffic is coming, let it pass. Look all round again.

5 When there is no traffic near, walk straight across the road.

Always remember to...

6 Keep looking and listening for traffic while crossing.

Learning the Code by heart is not nearly enough. The Code sets out the steps needed to cross the road safely. But for it to work properly, the child must understand how to do these things and why it is essential that he does them.

A Quick questions

1. What was the *Road Crossing Code* known as before it was improved?
2. Who published the *Road Crossing Code* pamphlet?
3. Who is the *Road Crossing Code* intended to be used by?
4. One reason for changing the *Kerb Drill* was that many children learnt it without understanding it. What was the other reason?
5. Should children who are too young to go to school use the *Road Crossing Code*?
6. How many safe crossing places are shown in the pamphlet?
7. What is another name for a pedestrian crossing?
8. What is the difference between a bridge and a subway?
9. What is the first thing to do after finding a safe place to cross?
10. If there is 'maximum visibility' at a spot, what are you able to do?
11. What are metal studs sometimes used for?
12. How should crossing places with studs be used?
13. Should you stand on the edge of the road while waiting to cross?
14. When should you cross the road?
15. What should you do while crossing?

B Think about it

1. What does 'setting a good example' mean?
2. What do you think is the best way to teach young children the *Road Crossing Code*?
3. Why is learning the Code not enough? What might children do?
4. What are the two essential things for a child to know?

New Words

Look at the words and phrases in the box below. Give the correct meaning of these new words as they are used in the passage. If you need help, use your dictionary.

kerb	code	publish	research
improved	pamphlet	volume	essential
studs	right of way	caution	maximum visibility

Language Practice

Orders and requests

A (Oral)

Read these sentences. They are orders or instructions.

a.
  Open the door.
  Write neatly.
  Cross the road carefully.

b.
  Don't open the door.
  Don't write untidily.
  Don't run across the road.

1 Now do this exercise in pairs. Look at the picture below. Albert is looking at himself in the mirror. He doesn't like what he sees. He tells his sister what is wrong. His sister tells him what to do. S1 is Albert. S2 is Albert's sister. Make up a dialogue between Albert and his sister. Follow the examples below.

S1: My face is dirty.
S2: Then wash it.
S1: I haven't brushed my teeth.
S2: Then brush them.

2   Look at the picture. Albert has cleaned and tidied himself. S1 is Albert; he makes statements about himself. S2 is Albert's sister and gives orders. Follow the examples.

S1: My face is clean now.
S2: Good, then don't dirty it.
S1: My shorts are mended now.
S2: Good, then don't tear them.

B (Oral)

Read these sentences. They are requests. Note: the first two sentences in table a. below are polite, the third is more polite and the last sentence is the most polite.

a. Please open the door.
    Open the door, please.
    Will you open the door, please?
    Would you open the door, please?

b. Please don't open the door.
    Don't open the door, please.

Now do this exercise in pairs. S1 must not look at S2's part of the exercise on page 90 and S2 must not look at S1's part of the exercise which is below.

S1 Look at the prompt words below. Make requests to S2, like those in table a., using the words given. Some of your requests must be polite (p), some must be more polite (mp) and some must be most polite (mtp). Listen to S2's answers. Write the number of his answer beside the word he uses, in the box below. Check your answers with S2 at the end. The first one is done as an example.

  1   (p) ... dust the table for me.
       S1: Please dust the table for me.
       S2: All right, but you will have to give me a duster.

2 (p) ... sew this button on for me.
3 (mp) ... open this bottle for me?
4 (mtp) ... wash this shirt ...?
5 (p) ... iron this dress ...?
6 (mtp) ... clean these shoes ...?
7 (p) ... cut my hair ...
8 (mp) ... knock this nail in ...?
9 (mtp) ... cut this cake ...?
10 (mp) ... put this screw in ...?

____ iron	____ thread
____ pair of scissors	____ polish
____ bottle-opener	____ hammer
1 duster	____ drill
____ spanner	____ polish
____ soap powder	____ screwdriver
____ knife	____ pin

S2 Listen to S1's requests. Look at the pictures below and choose one thing for each answer. Number the pictures: 1 for your first answer, 2 for your second answer, etc. Make sentences like those in the table below. The first one is done for you.

| All right, but you will have to give me | a spade. |
| | some soap. |

S1: Please dust the table for me.
S2: All right, but you will have to give me a duster.

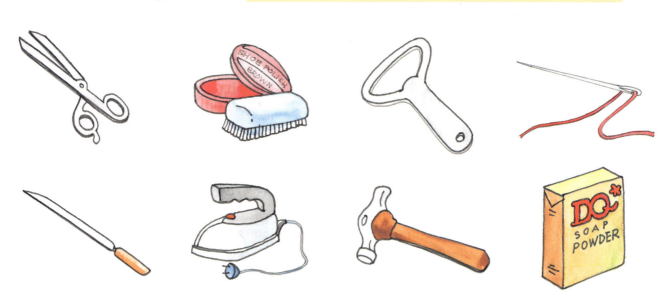

C (Oral/Written)

Read this passage. It tells you what happened when some new books arrived for the class library.

Paul opened the boxes. He cut the string with a knife. He did not cut his hand. He took the books out carefully. He did not drop any. He put them on the desks.

David looked at the authors' names. Then he arranged the books in alphabetical order. He did not get any in the wrong order.

Denis made a list of the books in an exercise book. He wrote them down in alphabetical order according to the authors' names. He did not leave any out. Susan made another list of the titles of the books in alphabetical order.

Jane took a pile of labels from the cupboard. She opened a pot of glue. She put a little glue on the labels and stuck them inside the books. She did not use too much glue. She did not get any glue on the covers of the books. She did not drop any glue on the floor. She was very careful.

Pretend that you are the class librarian and that you are telling the others what to do. Begin like this:

Paul, will you open the boxes, please? Cut the string with a knife. Don't cut your hand. Please take the boxes out carefully. Don't . . .

Verb pattern: *make*, *let*, and other verbs followed by the infinitive without *to*

D (Oral)

Read these questions and answers.

Q: | Did | your mother / she | let | you / him | watch television? |
|---|---|---|---|---|
| | | | | go out? |

A: | Yes, but | she | made | me / him | do / finish | my / his | homework / dinner | first. |

Now do this exercise in pairs. S1 must not look at S2's part of the exercise on page 92 and S2 must not look at S1's part of the exercise below.

S1 *Look at the pictures with prompt words below. Ask S2 a question about each picture like those in the table above. Then look at the box below the pictures. Listen to S2's answer and number the words he uses. Check them with S2 at the end. The first one is done for you.*

1

S1: Did your mother let you listen to the radio?
S2: Yes, but she made me write my composition first.

mother/listen/radio

2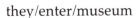
she/go/cinema

3
he/have/money

4
he/go into/swimming-pool

5
they/enter/museum

6
they/see/circus

7
father/play/tennis

| ____ ID card | ____ grass | ____ shoes | ____ shower |
| ____ ticket | __1__ composition | | ____ dishes |

S2 Look at the pictures below and listen to S1's questions. Give answers like those in the table at the beginning of exercise D, using the information in the pictures. Check your answers with S1 at the end. The first one is done for you.

S1: Did your mother let you listen to the radio?
S2: Yes, but she made me write my composition first.

E (Oral/Written)

Read these passages and then answer the questions in full sentences.

1 Last night at 11 p.m. Mrs Green suddenly heard a woman scream. She ran to her window and saw a man climb out of her neighbour's flat. She watched him run across the street and then she noticed a woman drive up in a car. The man got into the car. Mrs Green rang the police.

a. What did Mrs Green hear?
b. What did she do?
c. What did she see?
d. What did she watch the man do?
e. What did she notice?
f. What did Mrs Green do then?

2 Mrs Green eventually went to bed at midnight. She suddenly woke up at about 1 a.m. She felt something land on her bed and then she felt it move along the bed towards her. She turned on the light and saw a huge spider jump off the bed and disappear out of the door.

a. When did Mrs Green go to bed?
b. When did she wake up?
c. Why did she wake up?
d. Where did she feel the spider move?
e. What did she do?
f. What did she see?

Study Notes

to cross   to walk   to think   to try   to learn

All these are called infinitives. You have used them in sentences like these:

He wanted to cross the road.
She started to walk across.

After some verbs, however, the to is omitted. This is sometimes called the 'bare infinitive': cross, walk, think, etc. Two verbs used in this pattern are let and make:

The policeman let him cross the road.
The teacher made them walk.

Other verbs followed by the 'bare infinitive' are such verbs as saw, watched, noticed, heard and felt:

I saw him cross the road.
We watched her walk across.

Using a 'to-infinitive' instead of a 'bare-infinitive' is a common error.

Guided Conversation

Giving and refusing permission

Here are two ways of giving permission and three ways of refusing. In each case, the first way is the least polite and the last is the most polite. The words in brackets may be used or left out. In pairs make up dialogues like the one below about: the TV, the piano, the air-conditioner.

Request — Tom: Do you 'mind if I 'switch on the ↗ radio?

Permission — Ann: { ↘ No, I ↘ don't (mind).
{ ↘ No, 'not at ↘ all.

Refusing — Ann: { ↘ Yes, I ↘ do (mind).
{ ↘ Yes, I'm a'fraid I ↘ do. I'm 'trying to ↘ work.
{ ↘ Well, I'd 'rather you ↗ didn't.

Using English

Expressing obligation

A Mrs Morris is taking her class to visit a museum. She gives the class instructions about the visit. Read what she says and then write out her instructions. Two have been done for you.

> 1 You must be here by eight o'clock.
> 2 You must wear your school uniform.

Tomorrow we are going to visit the museum. Don't forget, you must be here by eight o'clock. The bus will leave at ten past eight and it won't wait for any latecomers. Please remember, you must wear your school uniform and you must all look neat and tidy.

Please don't forget the worksheets I gave you yesterday. Remember, you must make notes on at least five of the seven objects on your worksheets.

When you are in the museum, don't make too much noise and you mustn't touch anything. Also, please keep together.

Remember, the bus will leave the museum at twelve o'clock exactly, so don't keep anyone waiting. One more thing, bring a little money in case you want to buy a drink or something to eat. Remember, I want to see you all on your best behaviour tomorrow.

B Look at the five pictures below and at the top of page 95. Then write down who is speaking and what you think they are saying. The first one is done for you.

1

> The policeman is saying, 'You mustn't cross here.'
>
> Or: 'Don't cross here.'

policeman/cross/here

2

nurse/smoke/in the hospital

3

teacher/talk/in the library

4   5

mother/play/with matches   zoo-keeper/feed/the animals

C (Oral/Written)

Mrs Morris is going to take her class to a swimming-pool. Below are some notes she made of instructions she will give the children before they go. Study the notes and decide what Mrs Morris said to the class. Use what she said in exercise A as a guide. You are given some words to help you.

Don't forget to be ...

You must bring ... Also, please bring ... entrance fee.

You must ... into the pool. Please don't run ...

You must keep away ...

Notes

1. Be at school by 8:30.
2. Bring swimming-costumes and towels.
3. Bring 50 p for entrance fee.
4. Shower before going into the pool.
5. No running around the side of the pool.
6. Keep away from the diving-board.
7. No bumping into other swimmers.
8. Non-swimmers stay at shallow end.
9. Be ready to leave at 11:00.
10. Don't leave anything behind.

Guided Composition

First look at the example below which shows how you might begin giving instructions for doing simple, Physical Education exercises. Then give instructions for doing some or all of the activities listed below.

Stand with your legs apart. Raise your arms above your head as far as they will go. Bend down and touch the floor. Do not bend your knees. Raise your arms above your head again. Do this ten times. Next...

1. Doing daily exercises as in a Physical Education lesson.
2. Making something.
3. Cooking a meal.
4. Playing a game (making the correct movements not the rules).
5. Swimming.

UNIT 9

The Fastest Boy in the World

Eight-year-old world record holder, Wesley Paul, crosses the finishing line in a 10,000 metre run in Columbia, Missouri – Oct. 1977.

Do you know who this is? This is Wesley Paul, a Chinese boy who lives in America. The famous newspaper, *The New York Times*, has called him 'the fastest boy in the world'. Let me tell you why this newspaper said this.

Wesley was born in 1969. When he was three, his father started running every day, in order to lose weight. Wesley went with him! By the age of seven, Wesley was running 1.6 kilometres in six minutes four seconds and could run a 'marathon' (a race of 41.8 kilometres) in four hours and four minutes. A year later he reduced this time by more than an hour.

By the time he was nine, Wesley had taken part in six marathons and held thirty world records Do you know how big he was then? He weighed only 32 kilograms. Later he held *all* world records for boys aged seven to ten in all races from 1.6 kilometres to 41.8 kilometre-marathons. Experienced coaches now think that Wesley will one day be the first person to run a marathon in less than two hours.

Wesley was born with the body of a runner. His lungs can take in more oxygen than most people's and make far better use of it. But this alone would not make him a great runner. Very hard training is also necessary.

Wesley begins training every morning at 8 a.m. and runs for many kilometres. He does not run fast but every day he tries to run further.

'First you build up endurance,' he explained, 'and speed follows.'

There is no one near his age who can keep up with him, so he cannot test himself by racing other boys. Instead he competes with himself. He keeps setting new records. One year he reduced his time for the marathon by fifteen minutes within a period of three weeks. In a year he reduced it by more than an hour. It sometimes takes an adult marathon runner a whole year to improve by even ten minutes!

But running is not the only thing that Wesley is good at. His favourite subject in school is Mathematics but he also gets high marks in all other subjects. He likes to read science fiction and plans to be either a scientist or a doctor when he grows up.

'The people in my class ask me to race at recess,' he says, 'but I try to avoid it. I prefer playing games.'

Wesley enjoys being just another student... even if he isn't.

A Quick questions

Your answers need not be complete sentences.

1. Where does Wesley Paul live?
2. Which newspaper called him the fastest boy in the world?
3. How old is Wesley now?
4. Why did his father take up running when Wesley was three?
5. How old was Wesley when he began running?
6. In what time could he run 1.6 kilometres when he was seven?
7. How old was he when he first ran a marathon in four hours and four minutes?
8. How many records had he broken by the time he was nine?
9. How many marathons had he run by the age of nine?
10. Has Wesley run a marathon in under two hours?
11. In what way is Wesley's body different from that of most people's?
12. What time does he begin his training each day?
13. Why does he not train by racing with other boys?
14. In which subjects does Wesley get good marks?
15. What does he like to do in his spare time?
16. What does he want to be when he leaves school?

B Think about it

1. Can you say approximately in what time Wesley was able to run 41.8 kilometres when he was eight years old?
2. How old was Wesley when he held all world records for boys aged seven to ten?
3. What are experienced coaches (line 20)?
4. Can anyone now run a marathon in less than two hours?
5. What are the two reasons for Wesley being a runner?
6. How does Wesley train?
7. Try to explain in your own words what Wesley means when he says that his first aim in training is to *build up endurance*.
8. Who does he compete with when he is training? How does he do this?
9. What is so surprising about the results of his training?
10. Can you suggest why Wesley does not like to race at recess?

C Summary

Complete this summary of the passage by adding one word in each blank space. Some of the words will be found in the passage but not all.

Wesley Paul has been called the fastest boy _____ earth. He was born _____ 1969 and began running at the _____ of three with his father. _____ he was seven, he could run 1.6 kilometres in six minutes four seconds and a _____ in four hours four _____. At the age of eight he _____ his time for the marathon _____ an hour.

Before he _____ ten, he held all world records _____ boys aged seven to _____. One day he may run a marathon in _____ than two hours.

Wesley has a _____ body. He also trains very _____. He runs a long _____ every day to increase his _____. He is _____ trying to reduce his time and he has been more successful in this _____ many adults.

Wesley is also interested _____ school subjects and good _____ all of them. He _____ being a student.

New Words

Use these new words to finish the sentences:

| re'duced | 'records | ex'perienced | 'coaches |
| 'training | en'durance | com'petes | 'favourite |

1 By eating less, she _____ her weight.
2 The winner of the race was told that he had broken all the school _____.
3 No one can become an athlete without _____ hard.
4 His _____ hobby is cycling.
5 During the football match the _____ of the two teams watched from the side.
6 Someone running a long distance race often goes too fast at first but an _____ runner does not make this mistake.
7 He _____ in as many races as possible because he wants to gain experience.
8 Hard training is the only way to increase _____.

Pronunciation Practice

[ɒ] and [əʊ]

1

a cot   a coat   a knot   a note

2

A	B
got	goat
rot	wrote
rod	road
hop	hope
want	won't
fond	phoned

3

A

We are 'going to 'buy a 'cot for the ↘ baby.
It was a 'very 'long ↘ rod.
'When I ↗ left her, she was 'still
    ↘ hopping.
It was a 'very 'useful ↘ knot.

B

We are 'going to 'buy a 'coat for the ↘ baby.
It was a 'very 'long ↘ road.
When I ↗ left her, she was 'still
    ↘ hoping.
It was a 'very 'useful ↘ note.

Language Practice

Verb patterns with *ask*, *tell*, etc.

Look at the pictures below and read the sentence under each one. Then do exercise A on page 100.

Her age is 12.

His address is
22, Jordan Road.

The time is 4 o'clock.

The price of the
ticket is £20.

His height is 1.8
metres.

The width of the
room is 3 metres.

A (Oral)

Read these sentences:

He said,	'How old are you,	Betty?'
	'What's the time,	Peter?'

He asked	Betty	her age.
	Peter	the time.

Now do this exercise is pairs. S1 must not look at S2's part of the exercise on page 101 and S2 must not look at S1's part of the exercise, below.

S1 Look at the pictures below. In each picture one person is asking a question but you do not know who it is. Ask S2 questions beginning, *Who asked . . . ?* Write down S2's answers briefly in your exercise book. Check them with S2 at the end. The first one is done for you as an example.

S1: Who asked Mary her age?

S2: The policeman did. The policeman asked Mary her age.

(Write: 1 policeman.)

S2 Look at the pictures below. Listen to S1's questions. Give answers using the pictures. The first one is done for you as an example. Check S1's answers at the end.

S1: Who asked Mary her age?

S2: The policeman did. The policeman asked Mary her age.

B (Oral/Written)

Read these sentences then do the exercise on page 102.

1	The teacher Miss Lee	said,	'Take out 'Put away		your	books.' pens.'
			'Don't	write in play with		books.' pencils.'

2	The teacher Miss Lee	told asked	them	to	take out put away	their	books. pens.
			him	not to	write in play with	his	books. pencils.

Now do this exercise in pairs. Do <u>not</u> look at your partner's part of the exercise.

S1 Look at the list of people in the box and the picture below it. Then listen to S2's questions. After each question, look at the picture again. Decide which of the people listed in the box, S2 is talking about. Give short answers: *The guard*., *The porter*., etc. Then write the number from the list in the circle on the picture beside the appropriate person. The first one is done for you as an example.

> S2: Who said, 'Show me your ticket'?
>
> S1: The ticket-collector.
>
> (Write the number 7 in the circle beside the ticket-collector in the picture.)

| 1 inspector | 2 policeman | 3 policewoman | 4 porter |
| 5 luggage clerk | 6 ticket clerk | 7 ticket-collector | 8 guard |

S2 Look at the picture above. Then ask S1 questions beginning, *Who said . . .* and using the word prompts below. Listen to S1's answers and write them in your exercise book. Put a tick (√) beside them if you think S1 is right and a cross (X) beside any you think are wrong. Check them with S1 at the end. The first one is done for you as an example.

> 'Show me your ticket.'
>
> S2: Who said, 'Show me your ticket'?
>
> S1: The ticket-collector.
>
> (Write: ticket-collector √.)

1 'Show me your ticket.'
2 'Go to platform 4.'
3 'Stop.'
4 'Give me those bags.'
5 'Give me £10 more.'
6 'Don't take those on the train.'
7 'Stand in the queue.'
8 'Don't play in the station.'

C (Oral/Written)

Work in pairs. S1 and S2 take turns to say sentences like those in table 2 on page 101, about the picture in exercise B. Then write the sentences. Follow the example below.

> The ticket-collector told/asked the girl to show him her ticket.

D (Oral) Indirect questions – no change of word order

The students use the questions given to practise conversations like this:

> **Who invented the steam-engine?**
>
> Clive: Denis, can you tell me who invented the steam-engine?
>
> Denis: Yes, I know who invented the steam-engine. James Watt.
> Or No, I don't know who invented the steam-engine.

1. Who wrote *Robinson Crusoe*?
2. Who invented the telephone?
3. Who discovered penicillin?
4. Which land animal is the biggest?
5. Which animal lives the longest?
6. Which snake is the longest in the world?
7. Which country is also a continent?
8. Who uses a sextant?
9. Who is the tallest boy or girl in the school?
10. Which mountain is the highest?

E (Oral) Indirect questions – change of word order

Read the dialogues in the tables below. S1 starts the dialogue with a question. S2 doesn't hear S1 clearly so he says, 'Pardon?'. S1 then repeats what he said, but changes the word order. Then S2 answers the question. Notice, especially, how the order of the words changes in S1's second part of the dialogue.

S1:	What	is	your	full name?
	What	are		doing?
	When		you	going?
	Where	do		live?
	Who			admire most?

S2:	Pardon?
	I beg your pardon?

S1:				
	Tell me	what	your	full name is.
			you	are doing.
	I want to know	when		are going.
		where	you	live.
	I'm asking	who		admire most.

S2:	My full name is		John, Alan White.
	I'm	drawing	a picture.
		going	at six o'clock.
	I	live	in London.
		admire	my father most.

Work in pairs. Look at the questionnaire below. S1 and S2 ask and answer questions like those in the tables on page 101 to complete the questionnaire. S1 is given some prompts below to help him make the questions. S2 must answer truthfully and S1 fills in the questionnaire. The first one is done for you as an example. Take turns to be S1 and S2.

	S1: What is your full name?
. . . . . . full name?	S2: Pardon?
Tell me	S1: Tell me what your full name is.
	S2: (Give full name).

Questionnaire

1 Full name _____
2 District _____
3 Person admired most _____
4 Favourite food _____
5 Number of visits to cinema per week _____
6 Favourite film star _____
7 Number of hours listening to radio per week _____
8 Favourite singer/group _____
9 Favourite book _____
10 Favourite writer _____

1 . . . full name?
   Tell me . . .
2 . . . you live?
   I'm asking . . .
3 . . . admire most?
   I want to know . . .
4 . . . favourite food?
   Tell me . . .
5 . . . times a week . . . cinema?
   I'm asking . . .

6 . . . favourite film star?
   I want to know . . .
7 . . . hours a week . . . radio?
   Tell me . . .
8 . . . favourite singer or group?
   I want to know . . .
9 . . . book . . . like best?
   Tell me . . .
10 . . . favourite writer?
   I want to know . . .

F Indirect questions with *if* and *whether*

1 Read the examples and then change the sentences below as in the examples. In each case you can use either if or whether:

Is John coming?	I don't know if/whether he's coming.
Can the girls sing?	I don't know if/whether they can sing.

a. Is John coming?   d. Are the girls reading?   g. Does Mary play the piano?
b. Can the girls sing?   e. Can the boys swim?   h. Do the girls like cooking?
c. Is Mary reading?   f. Has John seen the Principal?   i. Are the boys careless?

2 In pairs, ask and answer questions like the examples above about your class-mates.

Reading for Information

There are almost three thousand languages in the world but only ten of them have a very large number of speakers. A quarter of the world's population is Chinese, but not all the inhabitants of China speak the official language, Mandarin. The eight hundred million who do are still twice the number of English speakers around the world.

The third most commonly spoken language is Spanish. Considering how small the home country is, it is quite surprising that Spanish has so many speakers. The reason, of course, lies in the colonial history of Spain. This led to the implantation of the Spanish language in most of Central and South America.

The spread of the English language is due to colonial and commercial factors. The great colonies of North America and Australasia were the commercial springboard which led to English becoming the most important of the international languages. French, once a close rival to English when it was the language of diplomacy, doesn't even figure in the top ten languages. It's international status, however, lingers on in the field of postal services.

Arabic has about one hundred and sixty million speakers and is the sixth most widely spoken language. It has the same number of speakers as Portuguese which owes its status to the fact that the biggest country in South America, Brazil, is Portuguese speaking.

The dominance of English as an international language is fairly safe. The Japanese adopted English as their language of commerce mainly because their own language is so difficult and they were dealing with the American market. The Japanese are rapidly becoming the dominant commercial power in the world and will probably continue to use English.

With the breakup of the Soviet Union and the reunification of Germany, the importance of German, already ninth in the league-table, is bound to increase. The Japanese have already taken note of this fact and more of their businessmen are learning German. They want to be ready to take advantage of the new European markets.

The Ginza Shopping District of Tokyo.

The top ten languages

	Language	Number of speakers
1	Mandarin	_____
2	English	_____
3	Spanish	_____
4	Russian	275,000,000
5	Hindustani	250,000,000
6	Arabic	_____
7	Portuguese	_____
8	Bengali	155,000,000
9	German	130,000,000
10	Japanese	120,000,000

1 Read the passage and complete the top ten languages table.
2 What position is your language in the table?
3 Which small countries have a language spoken by a very large number of people?
4 Why is English so widely spoken?
5 Why isn't the number of Japanese speakers likely to grow?
6 Which languages are likely to grow in importance? Why?
7 Which language has the largest number of speakers? Why isn't it a truly international language?
8 Why were Spanish and Portuguese so widely adopted?

B (Written)

Sequencing

1. Number the pictures in the best order to make a story.
2. Join the sentences under each picture using:
   and; but; so.
   Change nouns to pronouns where possible.
3. Write a paragraph for each picture using the sequencing words:
   First; Next; Then; After that; Finally.

a Peter and John went to a fishmonger's.
   Peter and John sold the fish for three pounds.
   Peter and John shared the money.

b Peter went to John's house.
   Peter and John went to the bus station.
   Peter and John caught a bus to the marina.

c Peter got up at six o'clock.
   Peter had his breakfast.
   Peter left the house.

d Peter and John went to a pizzeria.
   Peter and John ordered pizza, chips and salad.
   Peter and John had a good meal.

e Peter and John sailed back to the marina.
   Peter and John rented some fishing tackle.
   Peter and John caught a lot of fish.

f The bus arrived at the marina.
   Peter and John rented a small boat for an hour.
   Peter and John went for a sail.

Guided Composition

A (Oral/Written)

You are a reporter for a newspaper. You went to see Mr Long, a very old man, who lives in a little village. You wanted to write about him for your newspaper. He spoke a language which you did not know. His daughter acted as translator for you.

Here are the questions you wanted to ask Mr Long and his answers. Write out the conversation that took place. The first few lines are done for you.

Questions	Answers	Questions	Answers
How old are you?	Ninety-nine.	When were you married?	Seventy years ago.
What did you do when you were a young man?	I was a farmer.	How old is your son?	Fifty-five.
When did you stop work?	Nineteen years ago.	Where is your son?	In China.
What do you do now?	I grow flowers.	What is your son?	A clerk.
Why do you grow flowers?	I like flowers.	How old is your daughter?	Fifty-two.
How old is your wife?	Ninety-one.	Where is your daughter?	In Hong Kong.
Where is your wife?	In the kitchen.	What is your daughter?	A nurse.

Reporter: Please ask him how old he is.

Daughter: He wants to know how old you are.

Mr Long: I am ninety-nine.

Reporter: Please ask him what he did when he was a young man.

Daughter: He wants to know what you did when you were a young man.

Mr Long: I was a farmer.

Reporter: Please ask him . . .

UNIT 10

Stamp-collecting

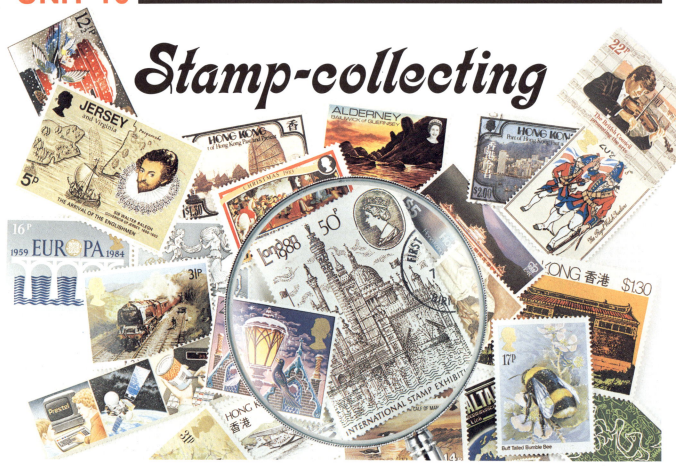

You will find stamp-collecting interesting because it will teach you a good deal more than just how to collect stamps. You will come to know the names of all the countries in the world; and you will find out something of their history, geography, and customs from the portraits landscapes or historical monuments engraved on the stamps.

If you are just beginning to collect stamps, it is a good idea to buy a small *packet* which contains five hundred stamps from all over the world. A *packet* is more expensive than a lot of unsorted stamps, but buying a *packet* is less wasteful in the end, because it has only one of each kind.

Stamps bought in this way are clean and ready to put into your album. But as you go on adding to your collection, you will get many dirty ones, and many with paper sticking on to them from the envelopes or wrappers they were attached to. Remove the paper and clean them at the same time.

How to clean dirty stamps

Separate the stamps that need cleaning from the others and soak them in lukewarm water until the bits of paper fall away. Dry the stamps on clean newspaper, but do not handle them more than is necessary. If any become creased during washing, moisten them again and dry them between clean white blotters under a heavy weight.

How to mount stamps

To mount stamps in an album use stamp-hinges, not glue or paste. Hold the hinge with the gummed side away from you. Fold about a third of it from the bottom towards you. Moisten this part and stick it close to the top of the back of the stamp. Stick the remaining part of the hinge to the space marked for the stamp in your album, so that the hinge does not show.

What to look for in a stamp

There are three things you will want to find out about a stamp:

1. The year the stamp was *issued*.
2. The *value* of the stamp. Even if you are not collecting stamps to sell and make money, you must know what they are worth because you will want to *exchange* stamps with your friends or with other people by mail. So you must know how much your stamps, and theirs, are worth.
3. If one of your stamps is a *sleeper*; this is a valuable stamp that has *accidentally* been mixed with ordinary, inexpensive ones.

Where to get information

You will find out just about everything you want to know if you look in the *Standard Postage Stamp Catalogue*, published by Scott Publications in New York. It contains pictures of all the stamps that have ever been issued, and information about them all. You will find the date your stamp was issued, and the value the catalogue gives, both to a new, and a used stamp of that kind.

A Quick questions

1. What is one way of finding out about a country's history?
2. What is sometimes pictured on stamps?
3. What should someone who is beginning a stamp-collection buy?
4. How many varieties of stamps are there in a *packet*?
5. Name one disadvantage of buying unsorted stamps.
6. Why can you put stamps from a *packet* straight into your stamp-album?
7. For how long should you soak stamps which need cleaning?
8. On what should you dry the stamps?
9. What should you use to mount stamps?
10. What three things should you find out about a stamp?
11. Why is it good to know how much your stamps are worth?
12. What is a *sleeper*?
13. What would be a useful book for a stamp-collector?
14. Where is this book published?
15. Why would this book be useful for a stamp-collector?

B Find out what these words in the passage refer to?

1. What does *their* in line 5 refer to?
2. What does *it* in line 14 refer to?
3. What does *ones* in line 18 refer to?
4. What does *them* in line 19 refer to?
5. What does *them* in line 21 refer to?
6. What does *in this way* in line 15 mean?

C Think about it

Put these instructions in the correct order.

1 To clean stamps:

a. Dry the stamps on clean newspaper.
b. Soak the stamps in lukewarm water.
c. Wait until the pieces of paper come away.

2 To get the creases out of stamps:

a. Dry the stamps between clean white pieces of blotting paper.
b. Moisten the stamps.
c. Put the stamps under a heavy weight.

3 To mount stamps:

a. Stick the bottom third of the hinge to the stamp.
b. Fold the bottom third of the hinge towards you.
c. Wet the sticky side of the stamp-hinge.
d. Hold the hinge with the sticky side away from you.
e. Stick the stamp into your stamp-album.

New Words

| 'issued | acci'dentally | luke'warm | 'moisten | soak |
| ex'change | 'portrait | 'landscape | 'monuments | 'value |

1 The artist painted a very lifelike _____ of my uncle which he liked very much.
2 The old railway station clock-tower is one of the town's most famous _____.
3 The first stamp, the *Penny Black* was _____ in 1840.
4 The _____ of certain stamps is increasing and, they are now worth a great deal of money.
5 Yuk Lan did not enjoy her bath as the water was _____ and she liked it hot.
6 There are some plants that you should only _____ when you water them. If you pour too much water on them and _____ them, they can die.
7 The mountainous _____ of Nepal is very beautiful.
8 Peter tripped and _____ knocked over a very valuable vase.
9 Very few shops will give you your money back for an item. Many shops, however, will allow you to _____ one item for another.

Pronunciation Practice

[ʌ] and [æ]

1

a cup   a cap   a lump   a lamp

2

A	B
cut	cat
bud	bad
run	ran
luck	lack
drunk	drank
much	match

3

A
He 'put the 'sweets in his ↘ cup.
'How did you 'get 'that ↘ lump?
The 'cut ↘ hurt her.

B
He 'put the 'sweets in his ↘ cap.
'How did you 'get 'that ↘ lamp?
The 'cat ↘ hurt her.

4 *Read aloud. The [æ] sounds are printed in red.*

a. He had already drunk three bottles. Then he drank another.
b. The doctor switched on a lamp to look at the lump on her forehead.
c. He ran until he could run no further.
d. He covered the cup with his cap.

Language Practice

Just, *already*, *yet*, with the present perfect tense

Look at the pictures below and read the sentences under each one.

1

S1: Has he finished swimming?

S2: Yes, he has just finished.

2

S1: Has he painted the door?

S2: No, he hasn't painted it yet.
He's going to paint it tomorrow.

3

S1: Ask Ann to cook the fish.

S2: She's already cooked it.

4

S1: Have the men finished digging?

S2: No, they're still digging.

A (Oral)

Read these questions and answers:

Q:

Has	Peter	fixed	the	fence	yet?
Have	you / the twins	cut		grass	

A:

Yes,	I have / he has / they have	already / just	fixed / cut	it.	
No,	I haven't / he hasn't / they haven't		fixed / cut	it	yet.

Now do this exercise in pairs. Do <u>not</u> look at your partner's part of the exercise.

S1 Look at the list of jobs below. At one o'clock you asked Peter, (S2) to do these jobs. At three o'clock, you telephone Peter and ask him if he has done the jobs. Ask S2 questions like those in the table above. Listen to S2's replies and, on the list of jobs, tick the ones he has done and put a cross beside those he has not done. The first one is done for you.

Jobs for Peter

1 Cut the grass ✓
2 Water the plants
3 Mend the fence
4 Fill in the hole in the path
5 Hang up the clothes
6 Paint the front door red
7 Fix the window
8 Repair the swing
9 Plant the tree
10 Put up the TV aerial

S1: Have you cut the grass yet?
S2: Yes, I've already cut it.

S2 Imagine you are Peter. At one o'clock, S1 asked you to do a number of jobs. At three o'clock S1 telephones to find out if you have done them. Listen to S1's questions. Look at the picture below which shows which jobs have been done. Give answers using sentences like those in the table at the beginning of the exercise. Check your answers with S1 at the end. The first one is done for you.

S1: Have you cut the grass yet?
S2: Yes, I've already cut it.

B (Oral) Reflexive pronouns

Read these sentences:

1

I	hurt	myself.
You	cut	yourself.
He	burnt	himself.
She	enjoyed	herself.
It	washed	itself.

2

We / Peter and I	washed / dried	ourselves.
You and Susan	taught / helped	yourselves.
They / The girls	enjoyed	themselves.

Now do this exercise in pairs. S1 covers S2's part of the exercise and S2 covers S1's part of the exercise.

S1 Ask S2 the questions below. Listen to S2's answers then look at the box of words beside the questions. After each of S2's answers, number the word in the box that he used. Check the answers together at the end. The first one is done as an example.

> 1 ... Peter ... at seven o'clock?
>
> S1: What did Peter do at seven o'clock?
>
> S2: He washed himself.

2 ... Mary ... at seven fifteen?
3 ... Mary and Peter ... seven thirty?
4 ... their mother ask them?
5 ... Mary reply?
6 ... their father ask them?
7 ... Peter reply?
8 ... Peter ask Mary?
9 ... Mary reply.
10 ... their parents tell them to do?

____ themselves	____ yourselves
____ myself	____ themselves
____ herself	____ yourself
____ ourselves	____ myself
_1_ himself	____ yourselves

S2 *Listen to S1's questions and give answers using the information below. Check the answers with S1 at the end. The first one is done for you as an example.*

> 1 (wash)
>
> S1: What did Peter do at seven o'clock?
>
> S2: He washed himself.

1 (wash)
2 (wash)
3 (dress)
4 'Have you both (wash) ...?'
5 'Yes, we've both (wash) ...'
6 'Are you sure you've both (wash) ...?'
7 'I've (wash) ...'
8 'Have you (wash) ...?'
9 'Of course I've (wash) ...'
10 'Their parents ... enjoy ... at school.'

C *Now use the information from exercise B to complete the passage below.*

At seven o'clock Peter ... At seven fifteen Mary ... At seven thirty they both ... Their mother asked them, 'Have you ...?' Mary replied, 'Yes, we've ...' Their father asked them, 'Are you sure ...?' Peter replied, 'I've ...' Then he asked Mary, 'Have you ...?' Mary replied, 'Of course I've ...' As they left, their parents told them to ...

Guided Composition

Note taking and changing speech to narrative

Mrs Green is talking to a policeman about a road accident which she witnessed.

Policeman: Did you see the accident, Mrs Green?
Mrs Green: Yes, I did. I saw it very clearly.
Policeman: What time was it?
Mrs Green: About half an hour ago.
Policeman: It's half past ten now. Where were you at the time?
Mrs Green: I was standing in front of the greengrocer's.
I was putting some tomatoes in a bag.
I heard a very loud noise. It was a sports car.
It was coming round the corner much too fast.
Policeman: What was the car like?
Mrs Green: It was red. I don't know what make it was.
Policeman: Did you see the registration plate?
Mrs Green: I'm sorry. I didn't. After the accident, I was too shocked to think about the number of the car.
Policeman: What happened then?
Mrs Green: A boy was crossing the road.
Policeman: Was he on the pedestrian crossing?
Mrs Green: Yes, he was. The driver tried to stop but he was going too fast. His car hit the boy. He didn't stop. He just drove away. By the way, how is the boy?
Policeman: His leg is broken but he's going to be OK.
Mrs Green: I am glad. I hope you catch the driver.
Policeman: Did you see him?
Mrs Green: Yes, I did. It was an open sports car.
Policeman: Describe him, please.
Mrs Green: He had long blond hair. He was quite young. He was wearing a blue jacket and a red scarf. He had sunglasses on.
Policeman: Thank you, Mrs Green. Let's go to the police station. I want you to look at some photos of cars. We must identify the make of the car.

Complete the policeman's report with notes. Use these headings:

> Time:
> Place:
> Date:
> Witness said:
> What witness was doing:
> Description of car:
> Description of driver:

Then write an account of the interview from the policeman's point of view.

Begin: I interviewed Mrs Green at 10.30 on (date). She . . .

Using English

Describing events in the past

A (Oral)

Work in pairs. Look at the pictures and the words. Decide what has happened. Follow the example.

cat/eat fish

The cat has eaten the fish.

1

man/cut/grass

2

boy/hit/thumb

3

girl/fall off/bike

4

woman/see/robber

5

man/win/race

6

girl/watch/sad film

7

aeroplane/land/airport

8

boy/read/funny book

B (Oral)

Work in pairs. S1 is from New Zealand and S2 is from Australia. You are travelling around Asia and have just met in Hong Kong. Each wants to find out which countries the other has already visited and which countries they have not yet visited. They do this by asking and answering questions like those in the sample dialogue below. S1 covers S2's part of the exercise and S2 covers S1's part.

> S1: Have you visited Thailand, yet?
> S2: Yes, I've already visited Thailand.
>
> S2: Have you visited India, yet?
> S1: No, I haven't.

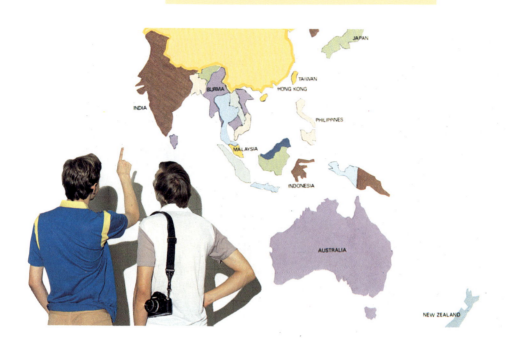

S1 *Copy out the table below. Then study your travel plan and fill in your part of the table. Now ask S2 questions like those in the sample dialogue above. Ask about all the countries on the map at the beginning of the exercise. Use his answers to complete S2's part of the table.*

S1		S2	
Countries already visited	Countries not yet visited	Countries already visited	Countries not yet visited

Travel Plan
Nov 7: Arrive Australia
Nov 11: Arrive Thailand
Nov 15: Arrive Burma
Nov 20: Arrive Hong Kong
Nov 23: Arrive Philippines
Nov 28: Arrive Taiwan
Dec 2: Arrive Japan
Dec 7: Arrive back in New Zealand

S2 Copy out the table below. Then study your travel plan and fill in your part of the table. Now ask S1 questions like those in the sample dialogue at the beginning of the exercise. Ask about all the countries marked on the map in the picture. Use his answers to complete S1's part of the table.

S1		S2	
Countries already visited	Countries not yet visited	Countries already visited	Countries not yet visited

Travel Plan
Nov 5: Arrive New Zealand
Nov 9: Arrive Japan
Nov 15: Arrive Taiwan
Nov 20: Arrive Hong Kong
Nov 23: Arrive Malaysia
Dec 5: Arrive Indonesia
Dec 10: Arrive back in Australia

C (Oral)

1 Work in pairs. Study the situations and expressions in the table below. Then match each situation with one of the expressions. For example, the first is: **1 b**

Situation	Expression
1 Mary has just passed her exam. 2 Susan is in hospital. 3 Paul has just stepped on Peter's foot. 4 David sees Mrs Lee carrying two heavy suitcases. 5 Mrs Lee has just thanked David for helping her. 6 Jane has just given Helen a birthday present. 7 Mrs Wilson has just returned from holiday. 8 Julie is going for an interview for a job.	a. Welcome back. b. Congratulations. c. Good luck. d. Thank you very much. e. Let me help you. f. I'm terribly sorry. g. Don't mention it. h. I hope you get better soon.

2 Can you think of any other expressions to fit the situations in exercise C?

Spelling

Read Spelling Rules 4 and 5 in Appendix 1.

1 *Give the -ing form of these verbs:* marry, strike, behave, travel, believe, welcome, fear, tunnel, begin, quarrel, love, carry, hit.

2 *Change these words into nouns:* lazy, happy, silly, crafty, crazy, shy, naughty.

3 *Change these words into adverbs:* clever, skilful, happy, gay, bad, bold, quiet, sincere, wise, heavy, noisy, continual, complete, practical, exact, merry, shy.

Revision Test 2

A Dialogues

Choose the best answer or response for each of the situations.

1 Your brother or sister says that he or she is going to turn on the radio. You do not want it turned on so you say:

  A Not!
  B Please not.
  C Not, please.
  D Please don't.

2 A young child has caught a bird and wants to keep it as a pet. You think it is cruel and you say to him:

  A Let it away!
  B Let it to go away.
  C Away with it!
  D Let it go!

3 You sit near a window in your classroom. Someone says to you, 'Do you mind if I open the window?' You do not want it opened and you say:

  A I don't want you to, please.
  B I'm afraid I don't.
  C I'd rather you didn't.
  D Yes, please.

4 A friend has just returned from a visit to the Principal to request permission to be absent from school. You want to know whether the Principal gave permission or not so you say to your friend:

  A Tell me what did he say.
  B Tell me what he did say.
  C Tell me what did he said.
  D Tell me what he said.

5 You are acting as a translator for your Arabic-speaking friend who is being questioned by an English-speaking doctor. The doctor says, 'Have you a headache?' You say to your friend, 'He wants to know . . .

  A have you a headache.'
  B if you have a headache.'
  C do you have a headache.'
  D whether you are having a headache.'

B Reading Comprehension

For each blank space choose the best answer from the choices given below:

Of all the things we eat and drink, water (1) the most important. Not (2) people realize this (3) it is quite true. The human body can go without food for a long time, but two (4) three days without water usually results in (5) .

Many people do not understand how (6) water the human body needs (7) work properly and many people do not drink (8) , especially in hot weather. Most people drink when they are (9) , but we often need more water, especially (10) we have been taking exercise.

A man's body is sixty-five to seventy-five per cent water. Water is very important in several different (11) . Most people need about five (12) seven litres of water every day, (13) we do not need to drink this amount (14) a lot comes from the food we eat. If we do not have (15) water, however, we feel tired and may become ill. Do you know what the best drink (16) ? Yes, you are right. Cold water!

1 A are
   B was
   C is
   D would be

2 A much
   B many
   C some
   D a few

3 A however
   B so
   C that
   D but

4 A and
   B or
   C but
   D for

5 A dead
   B fatal
   C starvation
   D death

6 A is
   B much
   C big
   D can

7 A to
   B for
   C so
   D and

8 A some
   B enough
   C too much
   D too many

9 A thirsty
   B needy
   C hungry
   D tired

10 A if
   B that
   C because
   D since

11 A manner
   B results
   C ways
   D needs

12 A or
   B and
   C to
   D from

13 A but
   B and
   C if
   D because

14 A because
   B and
   C that
   D or

15 A some
   B enough
   C that
   D all

16 A that
   B is
   C was
   D all

UNIT 11

Stop those Hiccoughs

There is not a man or woman alive who does not claim to know how to cure hiccoughs. The funny thing is, that the hiccoughs are never cured until they are ready to be.

So far, I have been advised to perform the following feats to cure hiccoughs:

Bend the body backwards until the head touches the floor and whistle in reverse.

Place the head in a bucket of water and inhale twelve times.

Drink a glass of milk with the right hand twisted around the neck so that the milk enters the mouth from the left side.

Jump, with the feet together, up and down a flight of stairs ten times, screaming loudly at each jump.

Lie down at the top of a grassy slope. Then roll down the slope and snatch up a mouthful of grass each time the body rolls over.

I have tried them all, but each time, at the finish of the act, and after a few seconds, one enormous hiccough always breaks the tension indicating that the whole performance has been a complete failure.

My latest failure came because I followed the advice of a doctor. It almost resulted in my being put away as a madman. 'All that the hiccough sufferer has to do,' explained the doctor, 'is to blow up an ordinary paper bag and then hold it over the mouth and nose tightly and breathe in and out of the bag instead of in and out of the open air.'

When I tried this, I made sure that I was alone. I blew the bag up and held it tightly over my whole face, like a mask. I did this for three minutes. I walked around the room at the same time to keep myself from getting bored.

When I removed the paper bag, I saw my wife and two children standing in the doorway. They were looking at me as though I had gone completely mad.

They did not seem to believe my explanation that I was walking around the room with a paper bag over my face because I was trying to cure my hiccoughs. I naturally felt very embarrassed

Incidentally, I still have my hiccoughs.

A Quick questions

1. What does everyone say that they can do?
2. How far backwards was the author told to bend his body?
3. When was he told to snatch up a mouthful of grass?
4. Did any of these methods cure the author's hiccoughs?
5. What was he told to do when he had his head in a bucket of water?
6. What was he told to drink?
7. How many times was he told to jump up and down the stairs?
8. What did he do every time he jumped?
9. Where was he told to lie down?
10. Where did the doctor tell the author to hold the paper bag?
11. Where did the author put the paper bag?
12. Why did the author walk around the room for three minutes?
13. Who was watching him?
14. What did they think when they saw him?
15. Did the paper-bag method cure his hiccoughs?

B

Find words in the passage with these meanings. You are given the line number for each word.

1. Not dead; living (line 1).
2. To get rid of (line 2).
3. To do something (line 4).
4. The opposite of *to straighten* (line 6).
5. To breathe in (line 8).
6. Bent (line 11).
7. Showing (line 22).
8. The opposite of *success* (line 23).
9. A lunatic (line 26).
10. To inflate (line 28).
11. The opposite of *interested* (line 36).
12. Took off (line 37).
13. Insane (line 40).
14. By the way (line 46).

C Think about it

1. How many things has the author done to try and cure his hiccoughs? Which one do you think was the easiest/most difficult to do?
2. Do you think any of them were impossible to do?
3. Why do you think he was nearly, *put away as a madman* (line 26)?
4. Why do you think he felt embarrassed (line 45)?
5. Have you tried or heard of any other ways of curing hiccoughs? What are they? Were they successful?

New Words

'hiccoughs	e'normous	expla'nation	em'barrassed
'tension	feats	in re'verse	

The author has tried many ways of curing _____. One of the _____ he had to perform was to whistle _____ while bent over backwards with his head touching the ground. None of his attempts, however, have been successful. The _____ of waiting to see whether his hiccoughs have been cured is always broken after a few seconds by an _____ hiccough. The last thing he tried was to breathe with a paper bag over his head. Unfortunately, his wife and children saw him and he felt very _____ as they did not believe his _____.

Pronunciation Practice

[ʃ] and [tʃ]

1

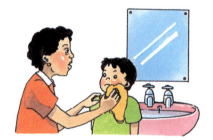

He is being given a wash.

He is being given a watch.

2

A	B
sheep	cheap
sheet	cheat
shop	chop
wash	watch
dish	ditch
cash	catch

3   Read aloud. The letters printed in red are pronounced [tʃ]. Be careful to sound the [t].

The children were having a cricket match on the beach. Charles was batting. Everyone cheered when he hit the ball right over the beach. It landed over near some hens with their chickens which had just been hatched.

Charles was not so lucky with his next ball. It seemed to catch the edge of his hat. John just managed to catch it. It was a very good catch.

Language Practice

A (Oral) Gerunds as subjects of verbs

Read these sentences:

Listening to	music	is	very relaxing.
Collecting	stamps		a popular hobby.
Eating		is not	allowed in the classroom.

Work in pairs. Look at the picture of Paradise Park below. You can see many notices which tell people what they are not allowed to do, but only one is clear enough to read. Below the picture are the Rules for Paradise Park but they are incomplete. S1 should look at the picture and say five things which are not allowed. S2 writes them down. S2 then says the five remaining things which are not allowed and S1 writes down what he says. The first one is done as an example.

Rules for Paradise Park

1 Fishing is not allowed.
2 _____ is not allowed.
3 _____ is not allowed.
4 _____ is not allowed.
5 _____ _____s is not allowed.
6 _____ _____s is not allowed.
7 _____ _____s is not allowed.
8 _____ _____ is not allowed.
9 _____ _____s is not allowed.
10 _____ is not allowed.
11 _____ a _____ is not allowed.

Gerunds as direct objects and complements of verbs

B (Oral)

Read these sentences:

> S1: Tom likes reading.
> S2: Then I'll buy him a book.
> S1: Amy loves watching TV.
> S2: Then I'll give her a TV set.
> S1: Bob likes sailing.
> S2: Then I'll get him a boat.

Work in pairs. S1 tells S2 what each of their friends likes. S2 tells S1 what he will buy each friend. Do <u>not</u> look at your partner's part of the exercise.

S1 Make statements like those in the examples above, using the prompt words below. Listen to S2 and write down what he will give each person. The first one is done as an example.

> 1 Ben (like) play – tennis.
> S1: Ben likes playing tennis.
> S2: Then I'll give him a tennis racket.
> (Write: *racket* .)

2 Ann (love) listen _____ to music.
3 Tony (enjoy) paint _____.
4 Helen (like) swim _____.
5 Jack (love) look _____ at the stars.
6 Jane (like) keep _____ pets.
7 Patrick (enjoy) cycl _____.
8 Susan (love) knit _____.
9 Paul (enjoy) collect _____ stamps.
10 Mary (like) grow _____ things.

S2 Listen to S1's statements and respond with sentences like those in the dialogue at the beginning of exercise B. You can choose your own words or use words from the box below. Write down the number of S1's statement and the word you use each time. Check them with S1 at the end. The first one is done as an example.

> S1: Ben likes playing tennis.
> S2: Then I'll buy him a tennis racket.
> (Write: *1 racket* .)

some wool	stamp album	kitten	hammer
telescope	some paints	plant	record
microscope	bicycle	goggles	book

C (Oral/Written)

1   Read these questions and answers:

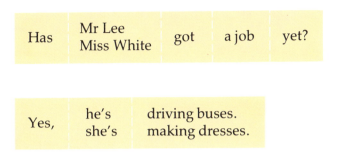

Note: he's/she's = he is/she is

Now do this exercise in pairs. Do <u>not</u> look at your partner's part of the exercise.

S1   Look at the list of names and jobs below. Ask S2 questions, like those in the table above, to find out who has which job. Listen to S2's answers and draw a line in pencil to join each person to the correct job. The first one is done for you. Check your answers with S2 at the end.

> S1: Has Mr Lee got a job yet?
> S2: Yes, he's cleaning windows.

Mr Lee	selling books
Miss Taylor	collecting tickets
Bob	cleaning windows
Linda	cutting meat
Mrs Green	making clothes
Denis	flying aeroplanes
Eric	building houses
Jim	playing the piano

S2   Look at the pictures and names at the top of page 126. Listen to S1's questions. Answer the questions with information from the pictures. Make sentences like those in the table at the beginning of the exercise. Check S1's answers at the end. The first one is done for you.

> S1: Has Mr Lee got a job yet?
> S2: Yes, he's cleaning windows.

2 Choose five people from exercise 1. Write two sentences about each person. Follow the example below.

> Mrs Lee has got a job making dresses.
> She is a dressmaker.

D (Oral)

Read these example questions and answers:

> Q: Is John's job making shoes?
> A: Yes, his job is making shoes.
>   He is a shoemaker.

> Q: Is Mary's hobby making models?
> A: No, it's making dresses.
>   She is a dressmaker.

Work in pairs. S1 must not look at S2's part of the exercise on page 127 and S2 must not look at S1's part of the exercise.

S1 Look at the pictures. Ask S2 questions like those in the examples above. Note S2's answers and check them together at the end.

S2 *Look at the pictures below. Listen to S1's questions. Give answers like those in the examples at the beginning of exercise D. Check your answers with S1 at the end.*

1 Paul
2 Mr Taylor
3 Ann
4 Mary
5 Mark
6 John
7 Simon
8 Mrs Lee

E (Oral/Written) Verbs followed by *-ing* forms

Read the first paragraph of the passage giving the -ing form of the words in brackets.

I shall never forget (go) to school for the first time. I remember (wake) up in the morning and (start) to get dressed while my mother began* (cook) my breakfast. She kept on (tell) me to hurry up or I would miss the bus. I soon finished (eat) because I was too excited to eat much. I was a very small child and I could not help (feel) very nervous. I kept on (wonder) if I would like (go) to school or if I would hate (be) a student.

Now read paragraphs two and three. Use verbs from the box in the -ing form to complete the passage.

| approach | cycle | travel | talk | work | write | think |

I remember that I enjoyed ____ to school that day because I was on a bus alone for the first time in my life. I have always loved* ____ on a bus though nowadays I prefer* ____. As the bus began* ____ the school, I started* ____ what my teacher would be like.

When I reached the classroom, all the other children were already there. They were practising ____. Some of them went on ____ but some of them stopped ____ and looked at me. Some of them began* ____ to each other.

Read paragraphs four and five. Think of suitable verbs to put in the blank spaces and write them in using the -ing form

The teacher told them to stop ____ and to continue* ____. Then she smiled at me and began* ex____ what I had to do. When she had finished s____, she showed me where to sit and I began* ____ my first work in school. It was easy.

'I'm going to enjoy ____ a student,' I thought.

Now go through the passage again using to *after every verb marked like this*. You can do this without changing the meaning.*

127

Reading for Information

A Following written instructions

Mrs Lee is moving to a new flat. Mr Miller is delivering her furniture today, but she won't be at home when he delivers it, so she writes a note to him. In the note, Mrs Lee tells Mr Miller where she wants him to leave certain pieces of furniture. Read the note Mrs Lee wrote to Mr Miller.

Dear Mr Miller,

I'm sorry but I won't be here when you deliver the furniture. However, could you please put the furniture in the following places:

The bedroom.

Please put the bed against the far wall opposite the bathroom. Then put the bedside-table next to it. Then please leave the dressing-table by the window, and the wardrobe between the dressing-table and the bedside-table.

The kitchen.

Please put the fridge in the corner by the door. Then the cooker must go by the window, next to the sink. The washing-machine can then go on the other side of the sink.

The living-room.

Please put the sofa between the two main windows. Put the two armchairs on either side of the sofa, facing the windows. Then put the sideboard against the far wall under the small window. Then leave the dining-table in front of it. Then please put the bookcase along the bedroom wall near the dining-table. Finally, please put the desk next to the bookcase. Please make sure that the bookcase is nearer the bedroom door than the desk is.

Many thanks.

Mrs Lee.

Now study the plan of Mrs Lee's flat. Each letter shows where a piece of furniture should go.

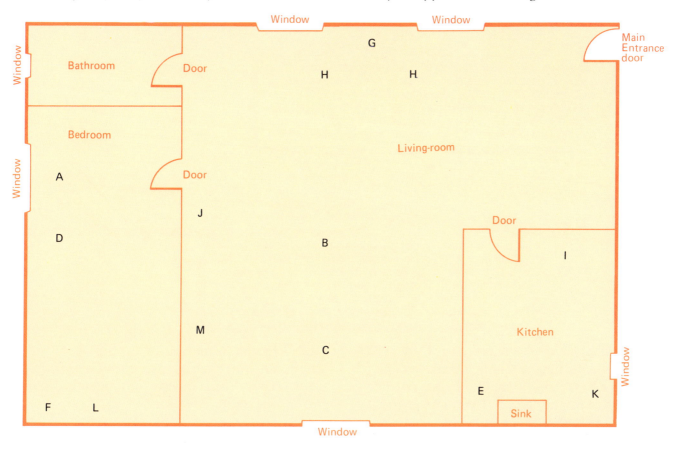

Copy out the furniture table below. Then read Mrs Lee's note again and match each letter in the plan above with a piece of furniture described. Now complete the table by writing a letter from the plan next to the correct word in the furniture table. The first one has been done for you.

Furniture Table

Bedroom		Kitchen		Living-room	
bed	L	fridge		sofa	
bedside-table		cooker		armchair	
dressing-table		washing-machine		sideboard	
wardrobe				dining-table	
				bookcase	
				desk	

129

B Using a dictionary (Verbs)

Study these extracts from the 'Oxford Student's Dictionary of Current English' and then answer the questions below.

> **Irregular forms** Whenever the forms of a *verb* (past participle, present participle, past tense) are *irregular*, these forms are given at the beginning of an entry in parentheses:
> **break²** /breɪk/ *vt, vi* (*pt* broke /brəʊk/), *pp* broken /'brəʊkən/)
> **drive²** /draɪv/ *vt, vi* (*pt* drove /drəʊv/, *pp* ~n /'drɪvn/)
> **fry** /fraɪ/ *vt, vi* (*3rd person sing. present tense* fries, *pt, pp* fried)

> **in-ves-ti-gate** /ɪn'vestɪgeɪt/ *vt* examine, inquire into; intake a careful study of: ~ *a crime/the market for sales of a product.*
> **in-ves-ti-ga-tion** /ɪn₁vestɪ'geɪʃn/ *n* [C,U]
> **in-ves-ti-ga-tor** /-tə(r)/, person who investigates.

> **steal** /stiːl/ *vt, vi* (*pt* stole /stəʊl/, *pp* stolen /'stəʊlen/).¹ take (a person's property) secretly, without right: *Someone has stolen my watch.* **2** obtain by surprise or a trick: ~ *a glance at her in the mirror.* **3** ◊ thunder (2). move, come, go (*in, out, away*, etc) secretly and quietly: *He stole out of the room.*

1   a. What is the past tense of *break*?
    b. What is the past participle of *break*?
2   Is the past tense form and the past participle form of *fry* the same or different?
3   a. What does *pt* stand for?
    b. What does *pp* stand for?
4   Complete these sentences using the correct form of the verb:
    a. Peter has _____ his ruler, so he can't use it. He _____ it at school. (break)
    b. Yesterday, the policeman _____ the recent murder. (investigate)
    c. The thieves have _____ my television. They _____ quietly into the house late last night. (steal)
5   a. What does *to investigate a crime* mean?
    b. What is an investigator?
    c. What is an investigation? Is *investigation* countable or uncountable?
6   a. How many meanings of *steal* are there?
    b. What are they?

Guided Composition

Use these notes to write a letter to a pen friend.

Begin: Dear . . . ,   *End:* Yours,

Try to join sentences with and, but, and then, because.

Paragraph 1: last weekend – went to London – stayed with aunt and uncle – had a very good time – aunt and uncle very kind people – weather wasn't very good – cold and raining

Paragraph 2: Saturday – went shopping – bought a new computer game – very difficult – Saturday evening went to theatre – saw Shakespeare play – very interesting – useful – studying it for exam

Paragraph 3: Sunday – got up early – went for walk in park – sun shining – had lunch – went to zoo – started to rain – got wet – saw lots of animals – panda – evening – watched TV – film about Antarctica – wouldn't like to go there – too cold

Study Notes

1. A gerund is sometimes called 'a verbal noun'. This is because it is in some ways like a noun and in other ways like a verb. You will remember that a noun can be used as the subject, object or complement of a verb:

   Subject — Object — Complement
   Football is enjoyable. I like football. My favourite pastime is football.

   A gerund can be used in the same way:

   Subject — Object — Complement
   Painting is enjoyable. I like painting. My favourite pastime is painting.

   But a gerund is like a verb as well because, like a verb, the gerund may have its own object:

   Painting pictures is very enjoyable. I like painting flowers. My favourite pastime is painting village scenes.

2. Some verbs may be followed by a gerund or an infinitive without changing the meaning. Examples of such verbs are marked with an * in exercise E:

   I started writing.
   I started to write.

3. Others may be followed only by a gerund:

   I finished writing.
   I could not help feeling nervous.

4. With some verbs the meaning is different:

   'Did you remember to post my letter?'
   'Are you sure?'

   'Yes, I remembered to post it. I didn't forget.'
   'Yes, I remember posting it very clearly.'

   You will have more practice with all these verbs later in the course.

Guided Conversation

Very polite requests and replies

Use your own words instead of the words in the box.

S1: Would you 'mind ′closing the ↗ door ?   S2: 'Not at ↘ all.

UNIT 12

SCOUTING

All Boy Scouts and Girl Guides know the name of Lord Baden-Powell. He started the Boy Scouts about seventy years ago. When he was a schoolboy, he was fond of spending his time in the fields and woods. He became interested in the little marks left by animals and people when they move about. This is called tracking and he became very good at it. (Soldiers and police often use this method to catch bandits.) Baden-Powell learnt to move so silently and carefully that even birds and animals did not hear him.

He found this very useful when he was a soldier in India and Africa. He used to go out alone, or with a few men, to look for the enemy and to try to find out their plans. This was called 'scouting'. He wore a wide hat to keep off the sun and carried a stick which was useful for a number of things. At night he used to find a place to camp. Then he made a small fire to cook his food and went to sleep.

When he came back to England, he made a very important decision. He decided to teach boys some of the things he had learnt. He wanted to teach them how to be useful, how to live in the open air, how to help other people and many other things.

He invited twenty-four boys to camp on an island with him. Some of the boys came from rich and famous schools. Others came from very poor schools. For two weeks they learnt how to live in the open air, how to track, how to cook their own food, what to do when someone is ill or has an accident, how to read maps, how to put up a tent, and many other things. At night they used to sit around the camp-fire singing songs and telling stories.

Then Baden-Powell wrote a book called, *Scouting for Boys* and soon, all over England, and then all over the world, boys wanted to become Boy Scouts.

Baden-Powell left the army and became the Chief Scout until he died in 1941 at Nyeri in Kenya. He arranged for groups of scouts to be started all over the world. Girls also wanted to belong to a scout group. Lord Baden-Powell's sister agreed to help him and together they formed the Girl Guides. Later the Sea Scouts was started for boys and girls who were interested in ships and the Air Scouts was started for boys who were interested in aeroplanes.

A Quick questions

Which of these sentences about the passage are true and which are false?

1 Lord Baden-Powell is now the Chief Scout.
2 When he was a boy, he liked being in the open air.
3 He knew how to move quietly.
4 When he was a soldier, he was often used as a *scout*.
5 When a soldier is used as a scout, he tries to find out where the enemy is and what the enemy is doing.
6 He invited the twenty-four boys to an island because he wanted them to become soldiers.
7 He taught the boys how to live in the open air.
8 He did not teach the boys to help other people.
9 Baden-Powell bought a book called, *Scouting for Boys* and gave it to all his friends.
10 For a long time no one wanted to be a Boy Scout.
11 England is the only country where there are Boy Scouts.

B Answer the questions below and on page 134 in complete sentences. The answers are begun for you.

1 What was Baden-Powell fond of doing when he was a boy? He was fond of...
2 What did he become interested in? He became interested in...
3 What did he become very good at? He became good at...
4 When he was a soldier, what did he go out to look for? He went out to...
5 What did he try to find out? He tried to find...
6 Why did he wear a wide hat? He wore it...

7 What was his stick used for? It was...
8 What did he decide to do? He...
9 Where did the boys who camped with him on the island come from? Some...
10 Where did they sit at night? They...
11 When Baden-Powell became Chief Scout, what did he arrange for? He...
12 What did girls then say? They said that they wanted...
13 What did Lord Baden-Powell's sister agree to do? She agreed to...
14 For whom were Sea Scouts and Air Scouts started? The Sea Scouts was started for boys and girls who were interested...

New Words

Make true sentences using these tables. Be careful. Do not make sentences that are untrue or not sensible.

1

We use	an umbrella / a sunshade / a tent / a shelter	for keeping off	the rain. / the sun.

2

Tracking / Finding out their plans / Waving flags / Taking messages / Washing away the soil	is one	way / method	of	catching bandits. / signalling. / passing information. / being useful. / tin mining.

Pronunciation Practice

A [tʃ] and [dʒ]

1

Jane is wearing a chain.

2

A	B
chain	Jane
choke	joke
cheer	jeer
cheap	jeep
rich	ridge
batch	badge

3

A
I 'think he's ↘ choking
The 'crowd 'cheered ↘ loudly.
I'm 'going to 'get a'nother ↘ batch.

B
I 'think he's ↘ joking.
The 'crowd 'jeered ↘ loudly.
I'm 'going to 'get a'nother ↘ badge.

4 Read these words aloud. They all end in the [dʒ] sound (not [tʃ]).

cage   page   charge   bridge   hedge   ledge   judge   dredge

B [aɪ] and [aɪə]

1

a tie   a tyre   high   higher

2

A	B
why	wire
buy	buyer
lie	liar
lies	liars
dry	drier
tied	tired

3

A
'What a ↘ lie!
'What ↘ lies!
The 'horse is 'tied 'out in the ↘ field.
The 'grass is ↘ dry.

B
'What a ↘ liar!
'What ↘ liars!
The 'horse is 'tired 'out in the ↘ field.
The 'grass is ↘ drier.

Language Practice

A (Oral) What... for? with gerunds

Read these dialogues then do the exercise on page 136.

1

S1: What's this bottle for?
S2: It's for ink.
S1: What's ink for?
S2: We use ink for writing on paper.

2

S1: What's this box for?
S2: It's for paintbrushes.
S1: What are paintbrushes for?
S2: We use paintbrushes for painting.

Work in pairs. Look at the pictures. Make dialogues like those on page 135.

B (Oral) Verb + preposition patterns

Read this passage and then complete the sentences below.

One day Peter happened to mention a story he had read in a newspaper about a haunted house near our school. He said that he did not believe in ghosts and most of us said that we agreed with him. Mary, however, said that she did believe in ghosts. When we laughed at her, she said, 'I'm sure that you all believe in ghosts really. If you don't, I dare you to spend a night in the haunted house. The house used to belong to a man who is dead now,' she said, 'and the house is empty. If you won't spend the night there, then you should apologize for laughing at me.'

'All right,' said Peter, 'I'll do it. Who will come with me? I can depend on you, Paul, can't I? Will you come, John? Can I rely on you to come with me?'

Paul and John said that he could count on them. The three boys decided on a meeting-place and tried to agree on a time. When Peter suggested eight o'clock, John complained of having a lot of homework to do and said that he might be a little late.

'Please wait for me if I'm late,' he said. 'I don't want to have to go there by myself.'

1 Peter happened . . .
2 Peter did not believe in . . .
3 Mary believed . . .
4 The others agreed . . .
5 They laughed . . .
6 Mary dared them . . .
7 The house used to belong . . .
8 Mary said the boys should apologize . . .
9 Peter knew that he could depend . . . and asked if he could rely . . .
10 John complained . . .
11 He asked them to wait . . .

C Complete these sentences with words from the passage on page 136.

1 While we were talking about football, he happened to _____ that his brother used to play for Egypt.
2 People said that the house was _____ by a ghost without a head.
3 'I _____ you to swim across that wide river,' the boy said.
4 'I must _____ for being late,' he said. 'I missed the bus.'
5 She _____ of a headache and went to bed early.
6 This rope will not break. You can _____ on it.

Noun + preposition patterns

D (Oral)

Read each sentence below and notice the words in colour.

1 They | quarrelled / had a quarrel | about who did the most work.

2 The two brothers | argued / had an argument | about the best way to paint the bicycle.

3 The Headmaster | spoke / made a speech | about keeping up the standards of the school.

4 The teacher | joked / made a joke | about Peter's high marks.

5 The woman in the shop | complained / made a complaint | about the price of the soap.

6 The police | inquired / made an inquiry | about the missing person.

7 I | strongly believe / have a strong belief | in working hard and playing hard.

Note: We use a preposition after the noun *discussion*: We had a *discussion about* homework. We do not use a preposition after the verb *discuss*: We *discussed* homework.

E (Written)

Read these sentences which are incomplete. Complete the sentences using words from the box below. Then use the missing words to complete the crossword. Note: A = across, D = down; 1A = 1 across.

| boxing | argument | comets | speech |
| decision | money | complaints | inquiry |

1. Mr and Mrs Lee often had quarrels about 2D . The trouble was that Mr Lee had a great interest in 1D and his hobby was very expensive. He could not see them crossing the night sky without a very powerful telescope. Mrs Lee made many 1A to her husband about his hobby but he refused to listen to them.

2. Peter and James had a long 7A about which sport Muhammed Ali was famous for. Peter won because he knew it was 5D .

3. 'Have you made a 6A on your topic yet?' 'Yes, I'm going to give a 4D on the topic of frogs. I'm sure the audience will enjoy it. I've already had one 3D about tickets.'

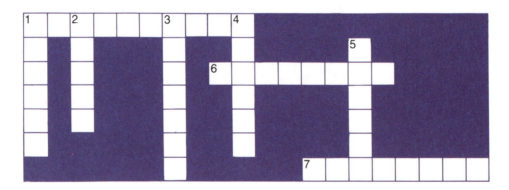

F (Oral)

Work in pairs. Make up dialogues like the example below. If you want to, you may use the words in the boxes below to help you.

S1: Are you good at anything?
S2: Yes, of course I am. Everybody's good at something.
S1: What are you good at?
S2: I'm good at avoiding work!'

| 1 frightened of |
| 2 ashamed of |
| 3 worried about |
| 4 interested in |
| 5 sorry about |
| 6 fond of |
| 7 pleased about |

| 1 stepping on a snake |
| 2 my handwriting |
| 3 passing the next examination |
| 4 making model cars |
| 5 not doing my homework last night |
| 6 eating sweets |
| 7 not having to come to school next week |

138

Adjective + preposition patterns

G (Oral)

Make sentences about yourself or people you know, using the words given:

| interested in | I am very interested in the history of this town. |
| good at | My friend, Tom, is very good at hockey. |

1 interested in
2 good at
3 afraid of
4 pleased about
5 excited about
6 sorry about
7 ashamed of
8 glad about
9 sure of
10 worried about
11 fond of
12 not interested in

H (Oral/Written)

Put in the missing prepositions:

When Peter and Paul arrived at the meeting-place that they had decided _____ (upon), John was not there.

'I was afraid __of__ this,' said Paul. 'He won't come. He *does* believe __in__ ghosts and he's afraid __of__ spending a night in the house. He didn't tell us because he was ashamed __of__ being afraid. He thought we would laugh __at__ him.'

'No,' said Peter. 'I don't agree __with__ you. I'm sure I can rely __on__ him. Let's not have a quarrel _____ (about) it. Let's wait _____ (for) him for another ten minutes.'

Just then John arrived and apologized __for__ being late.

'I'm sorry __for__ being late,' he said. 'Thank you __for__ waiting for me. I'm very excited _____ (about) what we're going to do. Are you both ready?'

'Yes,' said Peter. 'We were worried _____ (about) you, but now we can go.'

Guided Conversation

Expressing feelings

Work in pairs to make a conversation using the prompts given. Do <u>not</u> look at your partner's part of the conversation.

S1 Start the conversation with S2 by asking one of the questions, a., b., or c. below. Listen to S2's reply then continue the conversation by responding sensibly each time, using one of the alternatives given.

S1: a. What are you looking so pleased about, (S2's name)?
    b. What are you looking so excited about, (S2's name)?
    c. What are you looking so worried about, (S2's name)?

S2: ...

S1: a. What's wrong with him?
    b. What's exciting about that?
    c. What's so good about them?

S2: ...

S1: a. Where are you going?
    b. What happened?
    c. What did you get?

S2: ...

S1: a. Thanks, but I'm not very fond of camping.
    b. Oh. I'm disappointed with mine. They were less than sixty.
    c. Oh. I'm sorry to hear that.
    d. No thanks. I'm a little bit afraid of the sea.

S2: ...

S1: a. Oh, all right.
    b. Thanks.
    c. Good.

S2 Listen to S1's question and respond with either a., b., or c. given below and at the top of page 141. Continue the conversation choosing sensible responses from the alternatives given.

S1: ...

S2: a. My holiday.
    b. My Science marks.
    c. My brother.

S1: ...

S2: a. They are the best I ever had.
    b. He's in hospital.
    c. It starts tomorrow.

S1: ...

S2: a. Sailing with the Sea Scouts. Would you like to come?
    b. Camping with the Girl Guides. Why don't you come?
    c. Over eighty per cent. What about you?
    d. He broke his wrist playing football.

S1: ...

S2: a. Come on, you'll enjoy the open air.
b. Actually, it's not very serious.
c. Don't worry, you'll be quite safe.
d. Oh, well, better luck next time.

Guided Composition

(Oral/Written)

These drawings are the top and front views of the Sono FM/AM Cassette/Radio. Write a description of the two views explaining the position and function of the controls. If there are any you do not understand, discuss with your teacher. Your first paragraph might begin like this:

In the front view we see two microphones in the top-left and top-right corners. These are for making your own recordings. There are also two large loudspeakers, one on each side. On the top left there is the radio tuning dial and there are some lights. The lights on the left are for...

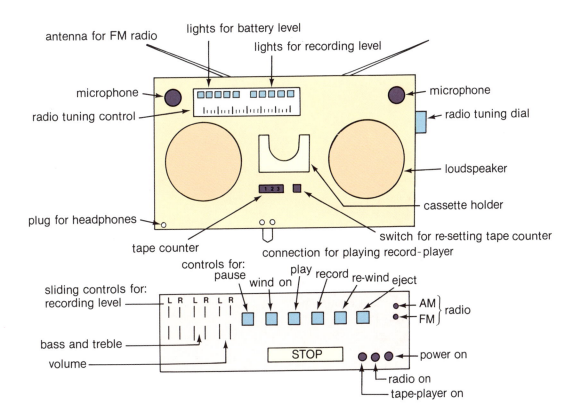

Using English

Finding out about others and giving information about oneself

A (Oral)

Work in pairs. Read the newspaper article below and notice what Bill Brown says the expedition needs.

Expedition Needs More People

Next month there will be an expedition to Nepal. The expedition will last for one month. The purpose of the expedition is to trek through the mountains of Nepal and to find out as much as possible about the birds, the animals, the flowers and the people of the area.

So far three people have been chosen to go on the expedition. The leader is Bill Brown who has been on many expeditions to Nepal and is an expert on birds. Jack Green is to be the cook because he is very experienced in cooking for expeditions in many parts of the world. The third member of the group is Jane Brown who is an expert on flowers. The leader of the expedition, Bill Brown, says he needs people with the following skills:

1. A knowledge of animals.
2. An interest in people.
3. Experience of climbing.
4. A knowledge of first aid.
5. A knowledge of photography.
6. Ability to get on with other people.

The expedition needs two more people and five people have applied.

Now study the information about the five candidates for the expedition. S1 and S2 talk about each candidate and then choose two out of the five to go on the expedition. The dialogue below will help you.

S1: Do you think Tom Lee is a good candidate?	S2: Yes. He is good at climbing and interested in photography.
S1: But there are six things on Bill Brown's list and Tom Lee only has three of them.	S2: He *has* been on an expedition before.
S1: Yes, but that was in the desert. Nepal has many mountains and can be very cold.	S2: I agree. The information also says Tom Lee is a very serious person and complains about things. Let's read about the next candidate.

The candidates				
Name	Age	Skills and hobbies	Experience	Other information
Tom Lee	16	Good at climbing. Excellent cook. Interested in photography and animals.	Went on an expedition to the Sahara desert last year.	A very serious person. He often complains about things.
Mavis Jones	17	Good at climbing. Fond of painting. Very knowledgeable about animals.	None.	A very cheerful person. She gets on well with other people.
Mary Green	16	Good at climbing. Fond of cooking. Very knowledgeable about flowers.	Has completed first-aid course.	A very organized person. She is rather impatient. Afraid of insects.
Raymond Sharp	17	Good at climbing. Fond of photography. Interested in people.	Has completed first-aid course.	A quiet but popular person.
David Brown	16	Good at climbing. Interested in people. Very knowledgeable about birds.	Went on an expedition to Australia last year.	A very serious person. He became ill in Australia but is now better.

B (Oral)

Work in pairs. Below are two tasks, choose either Task 1 or Task 2. Copy out the task. Now carry out the task by asking people in your group questions like those in the example. In the name column, write the name of the person you find for each item, if you cannot find anyone, write No one

> Are you good at singing?
> Are you a Girl Guide?
> Have you been abroad?

Task 1

Find someone in your group or class who...   **Name**

is interested in photography.
is good at table tennis.
is afraid of snakes.
is fond of playing football.
is a Scout.
has completed a first-aid course.

Task 2

Find someone in your group or class who...   **Name**

is keen on sailing.
is fond of camping.
is a Girl Guide.
is interested in birds.
is able to speak French.
has been abroad.

Now report your findings to the rest of the class. Make statements like these:

> Tony is fond of playing football.
> No one is my group/class is a Scout.

Dictation

When he came back home, he made a very important decision. He decided to teach boys how to be useful, how to live in the open air, how to help people and many other things.

He invited some boys to camp on an island. Some of the boys were from rich and famous schools, others were from very poor ones. For two weeks they learned how to track, cook their own food, read maps, put up a tent, what to do if someone has an accident and many other things. At night they used to sit around the fire singing songs and telling stories. Scouting for boys had begun. Later scouting for girls started when the Girl Guides was formed.

UNIT 13

Making Rain

One way of preventing floods may be by making rain! This may sound rather strange. As we know, heavy rain is the cause of floods, and in Malaysia most of the floods are caused by the annual monsoon, which brings heavy rain to the east coast. If, however, the rain could be made to fall in the China Sea, there would be no more floods since the rain clouds would not reach the east coast.

Is it possible to make clouds give up their rain? Yes, it is, and in 1973 the Institute of Scientific and Industrial Research (ISIR) suggested that it should be tried. The Institute knew of course that it is not possible to make *all* clouds give up *all* their rain. It calculated however, that if the frequency of rainfall could be reduced by ten per cent, and the amount of rain that fell each time could be reduced by fifteen per cent, the total amount of flood damage would be reduced by forty to fifty per cent.

As you probably know, clouds are caused by air containing water-vapour. The air rises and, since water-vapour becomes water when it cools, very tiny drops of water are formed. Since these drops are very small, they float in the air and form a cloud. When the cloud rises, however, the drops become colder. Because of this, they join together and become big drops. The big drops are no longer able to float because of their size, and they fall. As they fall, they pick up more drops and become bigger. This is the cause of rain.

Rain-making means making these bigger drops form and fall before they would normally do so. This can be done by 'seeding' the clouds with chemicals, like planting seeds in the ground. Rain can be produced in this way by three chemicals: sodium chloride (the salt we use on our food), dry ice, which is frozen carbon dioxide, and silver iodide. The seeding is done by aeroplanes which fly through the clouds.

The Institute said that sodium chloride was more effective when the clouds were warm, and silver iodide worked better when the clouds were very cold. For this reason, it was decided to use a mixture of sodium chloride and silver iodide.

The experiment began in November, 1973. The Royal Malaysian Air Force supplied a Caribou transport aircraft with special equipment to carry and release the chemicals. When the monsoon clouds appeared, about forty kilometres from the coast, the Caribou took off and flew through the clouds, seeding them with the chemicals. This took place at a height of about 3,000 metres. After ten to twenty minutes, the rain began to fall.

When the experiment was over, it was estimated that six aircraft would be needed. They would have to seed the clouds from Johore to Kota Baharu for three months every year. This would cost about US$20,000 each year. This is a lot of money but it is much less than the cost of the damage caused by floods. In times of drought, moreover, the same method could be used to make rain over land. Perhaps one day we may be able to control our rainfall in our country.

A Quick questions

Your answers need not be complete sentences.

1. What causes floods?
2. What causes most floods in Malaysia?
3. What would happen if the monsoon rains fell in the China Sea?
4. What happens when air rises?
5. What happens when a cloud rises?
6. What happens when the drops become big?
7. What happens as they fall?
8. What is the aim in seeding the clouds with chemicals?
9. How are the chemicals put into the clouds?
10. How do we know that the first experiment was successful?

B Think about it

1. Explain in your own words the two aims mentioned in the second paragraph.
2. Why was a mixture of chemicals used?
3. Why would it cost a lot of money to be effective?
4. Why would it be worthwhile?
5. Explain in your own words another way in which rain-making could be very useful.

C Summary

Complete the summary of part of the passage which is below and on page 148 by adding one word in each blank space:

In Malaysia floods _____ caused by the annual monsoon bringing rain _____ the east coast. There would be no floods _____ all the rain fell in the sea. The ISIR knew that this was _____ but it thought that it might be possible to reduce the _____ of times it rained and the

_____ of rain that fell each time. They thought the total amount of rain damage might be reduced _____ up to fifty per cent.

Rain is caused by air _____ water-vapour rising and becoming cooler. Tiny drops of water _____ and become a cloud. _____ the cloud rises, _____ drops become _____ and _____. They then fall as rain.

'Seeding' the clouds _____ chemicals makes these drops form earlier _____ they would normally do. The ISIR decided to use a _____ of sodium chloride and silver iodide. _____ November, 1973, an aircraft released these chemicals _____ monsoon clouds about forty kilometres _____ the coast at a _____ of about 3,000 metres and rain soon began _____ fall.

New Words

Choose the answer nearest to the meaning of the word as it is used in the passage.

1   'annual
    A   regular
    B   yearly
    C   monthly
    D   winter
    E   summer

2   'calculate
    A   work out
    B   guess
    C   think
    D   decide
    E   believe

3   'frequency
    A   amount that falls
    B   area covered by
    C   number of times that something happens
    D   speed

4   'normally
    A   always
    B   sometimes
    C   often
    D   never
    E   usually

5   ef'fective
    A   powerful
    B   successful
    C   easier to use
    D   widely used
    E   cheap

6   re'lease
    A   change
    B   spread
    C   let go
    D   move
    E   shoot

7   'estimated
    A   known
    B   worked out roughly
    C   worked out exactly
    D   finally decided
    E   announced

8   drought
    A   flood
    B   heavy rainfall
    C   light rainfall
    D   very dry weather
    E   storms

Pronunciation Practice

Read the words here and on page 149 aloud paying particular attention to the first two letters:

BL
black
blanket
bleed
blood
blow
blue

BR
branch
brave
bread
breathe
brick
bridge
bright
bring

broad
broom
brother
brush

CL
claw
class
clean
clear
clerk
clever
cliff
climb
clock
close
cloth

clothes
cloud
cloudy

CR
cradle
crash
crawl
creature
creep
creeper
crocodile
crop
cross
crowd
crowded
crush

cry
crying

SK
skin
skirt
sky

SL
slacks
slap
sleep
slip
slipper
slope
slowly

SM	SP		ST	
small	space	squeeze	stairs	street
smart	speak		stamp	strength
smile	speed	ST	stand	strong
smoke	spell	stairs	star	strongly
smooth	spelling		start	struggle
smoothly	spider		statue	
	spoon		steal	
SN	spread		storm	
snail			straight	
snake	SQ			
snow	square			

Language Practice

(*Not*) as... as...

A (Oral)

	Name	Age	Weight	Height
Boys	Peter	12	45.5 kg	150 cm
	John	13	43.2 kg	163 cm
	Charles	13	45.5 kg	150 cm
	Ben	16	50 kg	122 cm
Girls	Angela	10	27.3 kg	122 cm
	Helen	13	43.2 kg	132 cm
	Susan	13	43.2 kg	132 cm
	Mary	16	47.7 kg	163 cm

1 *Give short answers to these questions:*

a. Which boy is as old as Charles? John.
b. Which boy is not as old as John?
c. Which girl is as old as Helen?
d. Which girl is not as old as Helen?
e. Which girl is as old as Ben?
f. Which girl is not as old as Peter?
g. Which boy is as old as Mary?
h. Which boy is not as old as Helen?

2 *Finish these sentences about the children's weight:*

a. Peter is as heavy as . . .
b. John is not . . .
c. Helen is . . .
d. Angela is not . . .
e. John is not . . .
f. Susan is . . .
g. Peter is not . . .
h. Charles is not . . .
i. Helen is not . . .
j. Susan is not . . .
k. Charles is . . .

3 *Make as many sentences as you can about the children's heights.*

> John is as tall as Mary.
> Angela is not as tall as Helen.

B (Oral/Written)

Make sentences about people in your class using the words below:

1. as tall as
2. not as tall as
3. as short as
4. not as short as
5. as heavy as
6. not as heavy as
7. as old as
8. not as old as
9. as young as
10. not as young as
11. as cheerful as
12. as hard-working as

Reason using *-ing* words

C (Oral)

Read the example dialogue below.

S1:	I was so	angry with sorry for proud of	her. Peter. them.	S2:	Why?	S1:	For	being late. losing the money. coming first.
							For not	telling me.

Work in pairs. Look at the pictures and prompt words below. Make dialogues like the examples above. Take turns to be S1 and S2.

1. angry (break)
2. proud (win)
3. ashamed (not try)
4. annoyed (play music)
5. proud (help)
6. pleased (pass)

D (Oral/Written) *As, since* (= *because*)

Look at the examples. Notice that when a reason clause comes at the beginning of a sentence, it is followed by a comma.

| Because
As
Since | she had no money with her, she could not buy the book. |

| She could not buy the book | because
as
since | she had no money with her. |

Read the words in column A and column B. Match the beginnings of sentences in column A with the sentence endings in column B to make eight sensible sentences.

A
1. Since it's raining . . .
2. Because it was a holiday . . .
3. He can't play tonight . . .
4. As we've finished our work . . .
5. I'm feeling hungry . . .
6. Since it's getting late . . .
7. I couldn't sleep . . .
8. I felt really annoyed . . .

B
a. . . . the restaurants were crowded.
b. . . . because I missed the train.
c. . . . because I haven't eaten yet.
d. . . . we will take a taxi.
e. . . . I won't go out.
f. . . . because they were making a noise.
g. . . . as he's hurt his foot.
h. . . . let's go and eat.

E (Oral/Written) *Because of, owing to, on account of*

Read these questions and answers. Then do the exercise on page 152.

| Q: | Why did they | cancel
postpone
abandon | the | football match?
race? |

| A: | Because
On account
Owing | of
to | the | rain.
floods.
earthquake. |

1   Work in pairs. Do <u>not</u> look at your partner's part of the exercise.

S1   Look at the newspaper headlines below which are incomplete. Ask S2 questions like those in the table at the bottom of page 151. Listen to S2's reply and write the missing word or words in each headline. The first one is done for you.

a. **Fog – Planes Cancelled**

S1: Why did they cancel the planes?
S2: Because of the fog.

b. **... – Firework Display Postponed**

c. **... – Concert Cancelled**

d. **... – Tennis Match Postponed**

e. **... – Football Match Abandoned**

f. **... – Boat Race Abandoned**

S2   Listen to S1's questions. Give answers like the examples at the beginning of the exercise, using the words in the box below. Write the number of the answer next to the word or words you use. The first one is done for you.

a. S1: Why did they cancel the planes?
    S2: Because of the fog.

| _____ rough seas | _____ typhoon | _____ low clouds |
| _____ thunderstorms | _____ fog | _____ crowd trouble |

2   Now write five sentences like the example below. You may use words from the box or any others you choose.

They cancelled the football match because of the rain.

| cancel | postpone | abandon | boat race |
| marathon | meeting | basketball game | barbecue |

F (Oral/Written) *Due to, caused by*

Work in pairs. Take turns to ask and answer questions like the examples below. S1 asks S2 the question. S2 gives his own opinion using *due to* or *caused by* in his answers.

> S1: What are road accidents caused by?
> S2: Road accidents are caused by careless drivers.
> S1: What was the outbreak of typhoid due to?
> S2: The outbreak of typhoid was due to mosquitoes spreading disease.

1. What are swimming accidents due to?
2. What are headaches often caused by?
3. What is toothache caused by?
4. What is a sore back sometimes due to?
5. What is ill health sometimes caused by?
6. What are plane crashes sometimes caused by?
7. What is drowning often due to?
8. What are floods caused by?
9. What is disease sometimes due to?
10. What is his fitness due to?
11. What is fire sometimes caused by?
12. What is the poor television picture caused by?

G (Oral/Written)

Read these sentences:

Being	very rich,	he	had two cars.
Not having	a lot of money,	she	could not buy a house.
Feeling	very tired,	they	went to bed early.

Now read through the passage below. Fill in the blanks with the *-ing* form of the verbs as in the table above and with any other words you choose.

Danny and Eric left the cinema and stepped out into the street. It was late. _____ very hungry, they looked around for a _____ where they could have some food. Not _____ very much money, they wanted one that sold _____ food.

'There's one over there,' Danny said. They walked _____ the street but found the place crowded. Every _____ was full. Not _____ to wait, they walked further along the street. Round the corner, in a lane, there were some food-stalls. _____ no one sitting at them, Eric said, 'Let's sit down here and _____ something. There's plenty of room.'

'Too much room,' Danny replied. 'Not _____ any customers makes me think the _____ is not very good!'

Guided Conversation

Giving reasons

Work in pairs to make a conversation using the prompt words given. Do not look at your partner's part of the conversation.

S1 *Start the conversation by choosing one of the questions, either a. or b., below. Listen to S2's replies and respond using a sensible response each time, from the alternatives.*

S1: a. Are you angry with me?
    b. Do you feel sorry for me?

S2: ...

S1: a. For breaking my arm.
    b. For being late.

S2: ...

S1: a. It was because of a breakdown on the railway.
    b. I don't know what you mean.

S2: ...

S1: a. But I was in a hurry. I was late for school.
    b. The train stopped for an hour. It was due to a broken cable.

S2: ...

S1: a. I suppose you're right. I'll be more careful in future.
    b. No, they wouldn't let us because we were between two stations.

S2 *Listen to S1's first question. Then continue the conversation by responding with one of the alternatives, a. or b., each time.*

S1: ...

S2: a. Sorry for you? Why?
    b. Angry with you? What for?

S1: ...

S2: Not really,   a. I'm sure you have a reason.
                 b. I think it was your own fault.

S1: ...

S2: a. You shouldn't have stepped off the pavement without looking.
    b. What happened?

S1: ...

S2: a. Couldn't you have got off and taken a bus?
    b. That's no excuse for being careless. It's carelessness that causes accidents.

Using English

More comparisons; preferences

A *Rosie and Ben are talking about food. Read the dialogue and then copy out and complete the table.*

Rosie: What's your favourite food?

Ben: Indian food.

Rosie: Why do you like Indian food so much?

Ben: Because it's hot and spicy.

Rosie: But not all Indian food is hot and spicy. For example, North Indian food is not as hot and spicy as South Indian food.

Ben: No, it isn't. That's why I prefer South Indian food to North Indian food. What's your favourite food?

Rosie: I don't like hot and spicy food very much. So Chinese food is my favourite.

Ben: But some Chinese food is very hot and spicy. Take Sichuan food, for example.

Rosie: Yes, that's true. That's why I prefer Cantonese food to Sichuan food. It has plenty of flavour but it isn't as hot and spicy as other types of Chinese food.

Name	Favourite food	Reasons
Rosie		
Ben		

B (Oral)

Work in groups. Find out what each member of the group's favourite food is, and which is the favourite sport. Take it in turns to ask and answer questions like these below.

Q: Which is your favourite food?	A: Indian food is.
Q: Why do you like Indian food?	A: Because it's hot and spicy.
Q: Which is your favourite sport?	A: Football is.
Q: Why do you like football?	A: Because it's an outdoor game.

C (Oral)

Work in pairs. Study the table below which shows John's and Peter's favourite sports and the reasons why they like them. Now make up a dialogue between John and Peter. Use the dialogue in exercise A as a guide. You are given some help.

Name	Favourite Sport	Reasons
John	table tennis	1 Does not matter if you are not as big as the other player. Skill is more important than size. 2 Indoor game.
Peter	football	1 Outdoor game. 2 Team games are more fun than individual games. 3 Size is not as important as skill.

Peter: What's your favourite sport?

John: . . .

Peter: Why do you . . . ?

John: Because . . .

Peter: But you can't play it in the open air.

John: No, . . . That's another reason why . . . What's your . . . ?

Peter: . . .

John: Why do you . . . ?

Peter: Because . . .

John: Yes, in both . . . more important than size.

D (Oral/Written)

1   Study these facts then answer the questions in exercise 2 on page 157.

a. Ben did better than all the girls.
b. Ian came fourth.
c. Frank did not do as well as Jenny.
d. Susan came ninth.
e. Ann and Katy did better than everyone except Ben.
f. James came sixth.
g. Ann did better than Katy.
h. Margaret did not do as well as Susan.
i. Everyone except Donald did better than Susan, Mary and Margaret.

2   *Answer these questions based on the facts above.*

a. How many people are named? How many boys are there?
b. How many girls are there?
c. Did Susan do as well as Ann?
d. Did Ian do better than all the girls?
e. Did Katy do as well as Ann?
f. Did Donald do better than Frank?
g. How many people did worse than Susan?
h. How many people did better than Susan?
i. Who did the best?
j. Who did the worst?

3   *Now write out the order in which the people came.*

Guided Composition

Write three paragraphs on safety, giving rules and also giving the reasons for the rules. Here are suggestions for the paragraphs:

1   Safety in the home – using electrical equipment – fire – cooking stoves – hot liquids – slippery floors – ladders – knives – matches – young children.

2   Safety for pedestrians – crossing the road – using pavements – zebra crossings – traffic signals – getting on and off buses – policemen.

3   Safety in the science laboratory – (Notice the safety items in the photograph below.)

Test Paper

Part 1

Section A Reading Comprehension

For each blank, choose the best answer from the choices given below:

A vacuum flask can be used in two ways. We can use it to __(1)__ cold things cold or hot things hot. It is made so that very __(2)__ heat can get in from the outside or out of the flask from the __(3)__. __(4)__ you know how it works?

Heat __(5)__ in three ways: conduction, radiation and convection. Conduction takes __(6)__ when the heat moves through a material.

The vacuum flask has double walls made __(7)__ very thin glass. All the __(8)__ has been pumped from the space between the walls to make a vacuum. This is why it is __(9)__ a vacuum flask. Heat cannot move in a vacuum. Moreover, glass is a very bad conductor of heat. Therefore heat __(10)__ by conduction only very slowly.

The inside of the glass wall is 'silvered', __(11)__ a mirror, so that it reflects heat. As a result, not __(12)__ heat is lost by radiation. The flask is __(13)__ closed with a stopper so that practically __(14)__ heat is lost by convection. As a __(15)__, it takes a long time for heat to get into or out of a vacuum flask.

1. A freeze
   B make
   C keep
   D store

2. A little
   B few
   C some
   D much

3. A outside
   B air
   C centre
   D inside

4. A Can
   B How
   C Do
   D Why

5. A journeys
   B travels
   C burns
   D opens

6. A place
   B over
   C on
   D away

7. A out
   B of
   C in
   D on

8. A gas
   B air
   C water
   D inside

9. A considered
   B known
   C called
   D christened

10. A escapes
    B frees
    C loses
    D goes

11. A like
    B as
    C for
    D by

12. A few
    B many
    C much
    D little

13. A closely
    B tightly
    C over
    D fitted

14. A any
    B some
    C no
    D none

15. A result
    B reason
    C cause
    D therefore

Section B Dialogues

Select the best of the choices given for each of the situations. All responses must be polite:

16 When you get to school, one of your friends asks you, 'Who was that person I saw you with last night?' In fact you did not go out, so you reply:

   A No person.
   B I think you're mistaken.
   C I stay at home all the time.
   D I did not go back.

17 Your teacher picks up a bag which belongs to your brother and asks, 'Whose bag is this?' You say:

   A It is my brother.
   B My brother's.
   C It belonged to my brother.
   D It's my brother bag.

18 During a discussion someone says to you that in his opinion women should stay at home and not go out to work. You say:

   A That is not true.
   B I am disagreeable, I am sorry to say.
   C I'm afraid I don't agree with you.
   D You are talking a lot of nonsense.

19 You ask a shopkeeper for a dozen oranges but he gives you only ten. You say:

   A Not enough.
   B May I have two more?
   C Give me some more.
   D Can't you count?

20 You did not go to the cinema and this surprises your friend. He says to you: 'You didn't go?' You reply:

   A Yes.
   B No, I didn't.
   C Yes, I didn't.
   D Not really.

21 You wish to know the price of an article in a shop, so you say:

   A How much does that?
   B What a price?
   C How much is it?
   D What cost?

22 A doctor asks you how much you weigh. The answer is 55 kg so you say:

   A I am weighing 55 kilograms.
   B I have weighed 55 kilograms.
   C I am 55 kilograms weight.
   D My weight is 55 kilograms.

23 You don't feel well. Someone notices this and says 'Aren't you feeling well?' You reply:

   A No, I have a headache.
   B No, I am aching in the head.
   C Yes, I have a headache.
   D Yes, I'm not. I've a headache.

24 You answer the phone. Someone wants to speak to your father, who is at home. You say:

   A Please don't go away.
   B Hold on, please.
   C Wait a minute.
   D Please wait here.

25 You have never left your country. Your Geography teacher asks you, 'Have you ever been to Britain?' You reply:

   A No, I never.
   B I never go there, I'm afraid.
   C No, I've never been there but I'd like to.
   D Sorry, I had never been there.

26 You were practising a musical instrument with your music teacher when the phone rang. Your mother answered it and said that you could not come to the phone. The next day your friend asks you what you were doing when he rang. You reply:

   A I practised my music.
   B I was having a music lesson.
   C I was taught music.
   D I played some music.

27 You have a one-litre tin and a friend asks you what its capacity is. You tell him:

  A It is holding a litre.
  B It takes up a litre.
  C Litres.
  D It holds one litre.

28 The electric fan is off when your mother calls to you from another room: 'Please don't waste electricity with the fan!' You reply:

  A It's turned.
  B It's not.
  C I've already switched it off.
  D I've switched off it already.

29 You cannot avoid passing in front of someone who is looking at a painting on a wall. You say:

  A Excuse, please.
  B I wish to be excused.
  C Excuse me.
  D Am I pardoned?

30 You want to offer a drink to a visitor to your home, so you say:

  A May I get you a drink?
  B Are you liking a drink?
  C Do you like a drink?
  D Why don't you have a drink?

31 You have nothing to write with so you say to a classmate:

  A May I have a lend of your pencil, please?
  B Please borrow me your pencil.
  C Could I borrow your pencil, please?
  D Could I loan your pencil, please?

32 Someone says to you. 'How beautifully you write!' You reply:

  A Don't mention it.
  B Thank you.
  C That's not true.
  D Not at all.

Part 2

Section A Following instructions/Problem solving

1 Follow the instructions.

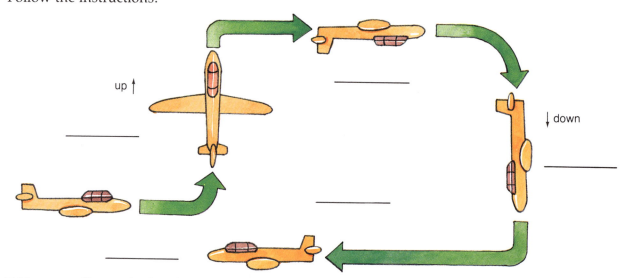

a. Write a small *a* on the line by the aeroplane when it is diving.
b. Write a small *b* on the line by the aeroplane when it is upside-down.
c. On the line in the middle, write the letter *x* if the aeroplane is flying in a clockwise direction. Write *y* if it is flying in an anti-clockwise direction.

2. Here is part of an advertisement placed in a newspaper by a large bookshop. It shows the usual price of each book together with its price if bought in the sale. Answer the questions.

Title	Published Price	Sale Price
Pirates	£9.50	£5.00
The New Book of Photography	£8.50	£4.50
The Complete Guide to Skin-diving	£11.45	£3.45
My Own Bumper Story Book	£5.30	£3.30

a. Which was the cheapest book in the sale?

b. John wanted *Pirates* and Mary wanted *The New Book of Photography*. They waited until the sale and then bought them. Who saved more money?

c. Mr Lee went to the sale. He bought *The Complete Guide to Skin-diving* for himself and *My Own Bumper Story Book* for his little girl. How much money did he save?

3. When Peter Green bought an electric fan as a birthday present for his mother, he was given this form to fill in. Look at the list below and choose the best items for the blanks (P), (Q), (R), (S), (T), (U), (V), and (W) in Peter Green's form. Write in the boxes.

SUNMASTER
GUARANTEE REGISTER CARD

IMPORTANT

POST THIS CARD NOW

This guarantee is void unless returned to us within fourteen days of purchase. Fill in all details carefully and mail to address on the other side.

Name _____ (P)
Address _____ (Q)
Tel. No. _____ (R)
Appliance bought _____ (S)
Name of model _____ (T)
Model No. _____ (U)
Date of purchase _____ (V)
Name of store _____ (W)

This appliance is guaranteed against mechanical and electrical defects for a period of 12 months from the date of purchase.

☐ FG/7410B
☐ August 1985
☐ An electrical appliance
☐ Peter Green
☐ Mr Lee
☐ The Oxford Department Store
☐ Oxford Street
☐ April 30 1960
☐ Electric Fan

☐ Flat 2, 124 Spring Road, London
☐ 'Whiz-Master'
☐ 20 August 1985
☐ £25.00
☐ 3 850827
☐ Spring Road, London
☐ Royal
☐ Passport No. C 234120

4. This table shows you how many pence per hour it costs to pay for the electricity used by a number of different electrical appliances. Answer the questions below.

Pence per hour (Approx.)		
4–7	Cooker	
5	Kettle	
5	Washing-machine	
1–3	Iron	
1	Floor-polisher Vacuum cleaner	
½–1	Television	
¼–½	Refrigerator	

a. Which of the appliances may use most electricity?

b. If it takes an hour to clean a flat with a vacuum cleaner, how much does that cost?

c. You switched on the television to watch a film at 9.35 p.m. The programme finished at 11.05 p.m. You then switched off. What is the greatest amount that this may have cost you in electricity?

d. Your kettle takes six minutes to boil. What does that cost?

5. Here is the face of a digital wrist-watch. Put the following in the boxes provided:

a. The number in the top right-hand corner.

b. The number immediately below the word AUTO.

c. The second word from the top in the top left-hand corner.

d. The number that refers to minutes.

162

Section B Reading comprehension

6 Read this conversation and then fill in each blank with a suitable word. Use only <u>one</u> word and write your answers in the space provided on the right.

_(a)_ you ever tried water-skiing? It is not as easy _(b)_ it looks! After a _(c)_ lessons, some people manage to stay _(d)_ the skis for a while, but some people _(e)_ manage to stand upright and have to give up.

Of course you should not try to water-ski _(f)_ you are not a good swimmer _(g)_ a water-skier spends a _(h)_ of time in the water, waiting to be picked _(i)_. You will find, too, that water-skiing is an _(j)_ sport because the equipment and the boat cost a lot of money. The cheapest way to water-ski is to join a club. Then you can _(k)_ equipment with other people. The boat used must have a _(l)_ engine because it has to pull a water-skier very fast, and sometimes it has to pull _(m)_ than one person at a time! The skis, too, are not cheap. They usually measure about 150 cm _(n)_ and 15 cm _(o)_. People _(p)_ are really good _(q)_ water-skiing often use one ski only.

(a) _____
(b) _____
(c) _____
(d) _____
(e) _____
(f) _____
(g) _____
(h) _____
(i) _____
(j) _____
(k) _____
(l) _____
(m) _____
(n) _____
(o) _____
(p) _____
(q) _____

Section C Interpretation of rules, notices, regulations, reports, etc.

7 The following explains how to play darts. Study it carefully and then answer the questions on page 164. One word answers are acceptable.

The game may be played by two people or by two teams. The players throw darts at a circular target which is divided into different scoring areas.

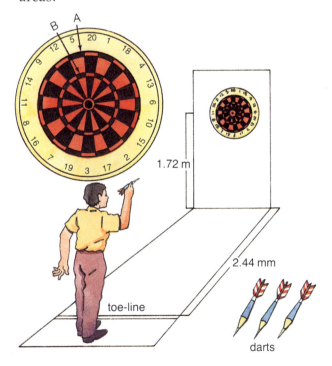

A dart in the smallest circle (the 'bull') scores 50 points. The ring immediately surrounding that scores 25 points. The scores for the other sectors are shown in the drawing but a dart in the outer ring (marked A) scores twice the number given, and a dart in the inner ring (B) scores three times the number given.

Players take it in turn to throw three darts each. They toss a coin to decide who begins. Players must stand at least 2.44 metres from the board when throwing.

A dart does not score unless it remains in the board when the player has finished throwing.

A number is chosen, usually 301. The aim is to deduct scores from that total until zero is reached. However no scoring can begin until a double number has been obtained. Moreover the player must finish on a double number. If a player's turn takes him past zero, he goes back to his score before that turn. The first to reach zero exactly wins.

a. What is the highest number to be seen on the board in the drawing?

b. What is the highest number that can be scored with one dart?

c. What number is scored by a dart that enters the outer ring in the number 18 segment?

d. If a player throws from a distance of three metres, will his score be counted?

e. What is the distance from the 'bull' to the floor?

f. What is the highest number that can be scored by one dart that does not enter the outer ring, the inner ring or the 'bull'?

g. A player throws three darts. They all enter sector number 20, between the inner and outer rings, but the second dart falls out before the third dart is thrown. What is the player's score for that throw?

h. A player has scored 281 and can therefore now finish with a double number. In which sector?

i. Instead of scoring double ten to finish, the player scored a single ten. What should he now aim for?

Section D Guided writing

Remember to write clearly. Answer both Question 8 <u>and</u> Question 9.

8 You saw a man attempt to steal a handbag from a lady tourist. You have been asked to write a report for the police in about 100 words. The pictures below show what happened. Write the report.

9 You have just received a letter from a pen-pal, David, in England. He says he has heard that most people in Cairo live in flats and he asks you to describe a typical block of flats. You happen to have a photo (right) which you send him. Write a letter to accompany the photo explaining the details and adding to them if you wish. You may also mention any feature of the flats not shown in the photo. Use your own address and the date of writing.

Appendix 1

Spelling Rules

Whenever you meet a new word, learn the spelling. If it is difficult to remember, copy the word out a few times until the correct spelling becomes a habit. Then make a note of it. You can keep a special notebook for this purpose and read the book through from time to time to make sure that you have not forgotten.

Spelling rules will help a little. Below are some of the most useful ones. Read the rules carefully. Then learn the spelling of the examples.

Remember that the vowel letters are a, e, i, o, u. The consonant letters are all the others.

Rule 1

A noun usually forms its plural by adding 's', but there are some exceptions.

a. Most nouns ending in 'f' or 'fe' change the 'f' or 'fe' to 'ves':

> loaf – loaves
> knife – knives

Other examples: thieves, leaves, wives, lives, halves, wolves, yourselves
Some exceptions: cliffs, chiefs, roofs, safes.

b. To form the plural of nouns ending in 'y', add 's' if the 'y' follows a vowel, but change the 'y' to 'ies' if it follows a consonant:

> toy – toys
> baby – babies

Other examples: monkeys, days, holidays, donkeys, countries, stories, flies, copies, ladies.

c. Nouns ending in 's', 'ss', 'ch', 'sh', 'x' or 'z', add 'es' to form the plural:

> atlas – atlases

Other examples: gases, circuses, classes, successes, addresses, guesses, churches, branches, matches, brushes, boxes.

d. Most nouns ending in 'o' form their plurals by adding 'es':

> hero – heroes

Other examples: volcanoes, cargoes, mosquitoes, potatoes, tomatoes, negroes, buffaloes.
Some exceptions: pianos, radios.

e. Some nouns form their plurals differently:

> teeth　feet　geese　children　men　women　mice　oxen

f. Some nouns do not change in the plural:

> sheep　deer　fish

g. Some nouns usually have no singular form:

> scissors　pants　trousers　shorts　pliers　news
> thanks　tongs　measles　goods　means

h. Learn these noun plurals: sons-in-law, passers-by.

Rule 2

Words ending in 'e' usually drop the 'e' before a vowel, but keep it before a consonant:

> love – lovable, loving, lovely

a. Other examples: moving, moved, hoping, dared, shaped, smiling, causing, exciting.
   Note:

> hope – hoping;　　hop – hopping
> file – filing;　　 fill – filling
> scrape – scraping;　scrap – scrapping

b. Some words do not drop the 'e' before a vowel.

   Some examples: eye – eyeing, agree – agreeable, peace – peaceable, marriage – marriageable, mile – mileage, dye – dyeing.

c. Some words do drop the 'e' before a consonant:

> true – truly　　whole – wholly　　argue – argument

Rule 3

a. When the sound is *ee* [iː] 'i' comes before 'e', except after 'c':
   piece (the sound is *ee* and it does not come after 'c'),
   deceive (the sound is *ee* but it comes after 'c').

   Other examples: grief, belief, believe, achieve, besiege, relieve, conceit, receive, deceit, ceiling, receipt.

   Some exceptions: seize, weird.

b. In these words the sound is not *ee*: weight, reign, neighbour, their, leisure.

Rule 4

Words ending in 'y' keeping the 'y' before 'ing' when forming *-ing* words.

carrying   buying   marrying   denying   relying

Rule 5

Words ending in 'y' change the 'y' into 'i':

a. before adding 'ly' to form adverbs:
Some examples: prettily, happily, merrily, heavily, gaily, tidily.
Some exceptions: slyly, shyly.

b. when forming nouns like these:

happiness   business   loneliness   silliness   naughtiness

Some exceptions: slyness, dryness, shyness, annoyance.

Rule 6

When the words 'all' and 'full' are used to make up longer words, one 'l' is dropped.

Some examples: always, altogether, although, almost, almighty, already, also, alone, careful, cheerful, doubtful, thoughtful, hopeful, peaceful, tuneful, fearful.

Note: Other words ending in 'll' used to make up longer words, sometimes drop one 'l' and sometimes keep it.

Learn the spelling of the following:
a. skilful, until, welfare, welcome, enrol.
b. unroll, illwill, farewell, recall, befall, downfall, smallness, all right.

Rule 7

A word ending in a consonant keeps the consonant when '-ness' or '-ly' is added.

Some examples: keenness, meanness, cleanness, thinness, really, hopefully, gracefully, specially, truthfully, fearfully, totally, finally.

Rule 8

When adding 'dis' and 'mis' to other words, the 's' is always kept, even if the other words begin with an 's':

dis – appear, disappear
mis – take, mistake
mis – spell, misspell

Other examples: disappoint, disqualify, disagree, dissolve, dissect, mistrust, misuse.

Rule 9

A word of one syllable containing a short vowel and ending in one consonant, doubles this consonant when another syllable beginning with a vowel is added:

> sad – sadder – sadly

a. Some examples of adding 'er', 'ed', or 'ing':

blotter, blotting, blotted, batting, runner, running, chopping, tapped, shutting, cutter, slipped, supper, mapped, skipping, flipper, nipped, sipping, dabbed.

b. Some examples of adding 'y' (which at the end of a word may be thought of as a vowel):

> sunny   funny   floppy   gritty

Rule 10

A word ending in one vowel followed by 'l', doubles the 'l', when a syllable beginning with a vowel is added:

> expel – expelling, expelled
> reveal – revealing (two vowels)

Other examples: quarrelling, travelled, marvellous, propelling, concealed.

Note: dial – dialling, equal – equalling.

Rule 11

A word of two or three syllables ending in *one* vowel and a consonant, doubles the consonant when a syllable beginning with a vowel is added, *if the second syllable is stressed*:

beGIN – beginning (one vowel, one consonant, second syllable stressed)
Open – opening (one vowel, one consonant but first syllable stressed)
sucCEED – succeeding (second syllable stressed but two vowels)
comMIT – commitment (one vowel, second syllable stressed, but the syllable added begins with a consonant).

Other examples: committing, mattering, appearing, regretting, occurring, permitting, transferring, appealing.

An exception: transferable.

Rule 12

An 'e' after a 'c' or 'g' makes these letters soft: e.g. 'rag' becomes 'rage'. The 'e' is not necessary before a syllable beginning with 'e' or 'i', but it is kept before a syllable beginning with 'a' or 'o':

> notice   noticing   noticeable

Other examples: serviced, servicing, serviceable; managed, managing, manageable; changed, changing, changeable; pronounced, pronouncing, pronounceable; peaceable, traceable, courageous; encouraging.

Appendix 2

Grammar Summary And Practice

A Relative pronouns

who, which, whose

who is used for people
e.g. That's the man who stole the car.

whose is also used for people
e.g. That's the man whose car was stolen.

which is used for animals and things.
e.g. That's the dog which bit the man.
     That's the car which the man stole.

Complete these sentences with relative pronouns

1 It was Peter _____ won the race.
2 I don't know _____ book this is.
3 That's the car _____ was stolen.
4 The teacher spoke to the children _____ were making too much noise.
5 The train, _____ arrived late, was full.
6 There's a man, _____ name I don't know, at the door.

B Reflexive pronouns

> myself;   yourself;   himself;   herself;   ourselves;   themselves

e.g. You only have yourself to blame.
     I'll decorate the house myself.

Complete these sentences with reflexive pronouns

1 I helped Sam with his homework because he couldn't do it himself.
2 If you are hungry, Tom, help _____ to a sandwich.
3 People have to serve _____ in self-service restaurants.
4 I _____ have seen several accidents today.
5 We have to help _____ when there is no-one else to help.
6 Mary looked at _____ in the mirror.

C Indefinite quantities

many, a few, a lot of, too many,
are used with countable nouns.

You can't have too many books.

much, a little, a lot of, too much,
are used with uncountable nouns.

She bought too much milk and it went sour.

Complete these sentences:

1 _____ people in third world countries only have _____ to eat.
2 If we all gave _____ pounds to charity _____ lives would be saved.
3 In the developed countries _____ people eat _____ food.

170

D Comparative and superlative of adjectives

Look at this example

John is tall.
He's taller than Peter.
He's the tallest boy in his class.

There are several different spelling patterns.

1. Some adjectives add -er -est.
   e.g. short   shorter   shortest
   strong   stronger   strongest
2. Some double the last consonant.
   e.g. fat   fatter   fattest
   thin   thinner   thinnest
3. A final -y becomes an -i.
   e.g. happy   happier   happiest
   heavy   heavier   heaviest
4. A final -e is dropped
   e.g. nice   nicer   nicest
   cute   cuter   cutest
5. Longer adjectives use *more* and *most*.
   e.g. beautiful   more beautiful   most beautiful
   intelligent   more intelligent   most intelligent
6. Some adjectives are irregular
   e.g. good   better   best
   bad   worse   worst

Complete these sentences

1. The World Trade Center is the _____ building in New York.
2. Peter weighs 40 kilos. At 45 kilos John is 5 kilos _____.
3. Their house is nice but our house is _____.
4. Peter's father was angry because his son had the _____ marks in the exam.
5. John is intelligent but he isn't the _____ boy in his class.

E The Present Simple and Present Continuous Tenses

Look at this example:

Ann eats an apple every day. (simple present)
She's eating an apple now. (present continuous)

The present continuous tense refers to actions which are happening now.

Put the (verbs) in the simple present or present continuous tense:

Ann usually (go) to school on the bus but today she (walk) with her friend, Susan.
Ann and Susan (play) tennis and Susan (need) a new racket.
Now the girls (look) in the window of a sports shop.
Ann (see) a racket she can afford so she (go) in and (buy) it.
It's now five o'clock and the sun (set).
The girls (come) onto the tennis court to play.
Susan (use) her new racket, of course, and she (think) she is going to win.

F The Simple Past and Present Perfect Tenses

The simple past tense shows when something has happened.
The present perfect tense shows that an activity is completed now. It does not tell us when.

Put the (verbs) in the simple past or present perfect tense.

1 I (be) to Damascus several times. I (go) there twice last year.
2 Peter (lose) the book which he (borrow) from John last week.
3 He doesn't want to see the film because he (read) the book.
4 Susan is happy because she (finish) her homework.
5 Many people (climb) Everest since Hillary (climb) it in 1953.

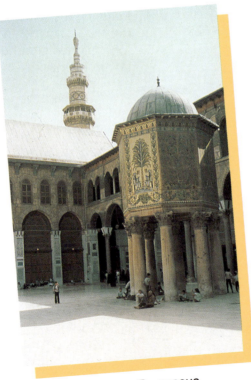

Omayyed Mosque, Damascus.

G The Gerund

This is sometimes called a verb-noun.

Here are some examples:

Verb: to swim. *Gerund:* swimming

I like swimming.
Swimming is good exercise.

Change the verbs to gerunds:

1. (Fish) and (cycle) are popular pastimes.
2. Susan's favourite pastimes are (talk) and (listen) to records.
3. Athletics consists of (run), (jump) and (throw) events.
4. (Read) and (write) are vital skills.

Appendix 3

Phonetic Symbols

Consonants		Consonants		Vowels		Diphthongs	
b	bag	p	pen	æ –	black	aɪ –	my
d	desk	r	ruler	ɑː –	arm	aʊ –	mouth
dʒ	jar	s	saucer	ə –	ruler	eɪ –	table
f	fan	ʃ	ship		– a book	əʊ –	nose
g	girl	t	table	ɜː –	bird	ɔɪ –	boy
h	hen	tʃ	chair	e –	pen	ɪə –	here
j	yes	θ	thin	ɪ –	pig	eə –	hair
k	cat	ð	that	iː –	green	ʊə –	sure
l	leg	v	village	ɒ –	dog		
m	man	w	window	ɔː –	saw		
n	nose	z	zoo	ʊ –	book		
ŋ	string	ʒ	measure	uː –	ruler		
				ʌ –	cup		

1 A tour of the Universe

What is a planet?
▼ A **planet** is a body which spins around a star. The **Earth** is a planet.

What is a moon?
▼ A **moon** is a body Earth has one moon.

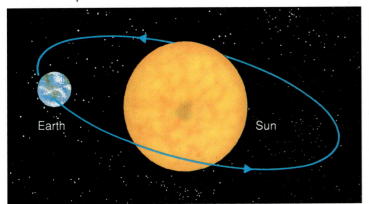
Earth — Sun

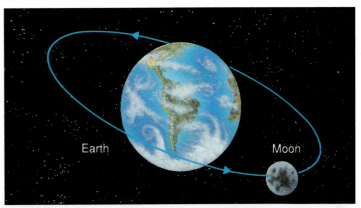
Earth — Moon

What is a solar system?
▶ The Earth is just one of nine planets, at least 41 moons and thousands of **asteroids** and **comets** which spin around our **Sun** and make up our **Solar System**.

What is a star?
▶ A **star** is a large body which produces its own energy. Our Sun is a star. It is at the centre of our Solar System.

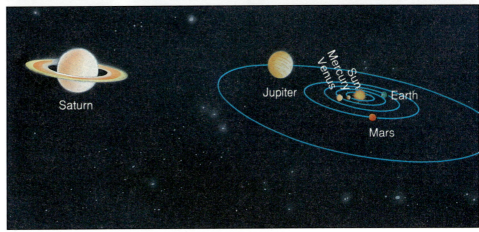
Saturn, Jupiter, Mercury, Venus, Sun, Earth, Mars

What is a galaxy?
▼ The Solar System and all the stars that you see at night make up our **galaxy**. It is called **The Milky Way**.

What is the Universe?
▼ The **Universe** contains millions of galaxies. It contains everything that exists.

YOU ARE HERE

Q1 What is a planet?	**Q3** What is a star?	**Q5** List five things that you would find in a galaxy.
Q2 What is a moon?	**Q4** How many planets are there in our Solar System?	

2 The Earth

Is the Earth flat or round?

For thousands of years people thought the Earth was flat. In this experiment you are going to look at some of the reasons why people changed their minds and agreed that it was shaped like a ball.

Apparatus

- card ☐ sticky tape ☐ string
- torch ☐ 2 balls of Plasticine
- paper boat ☐ 2 knitting needles
- 2 clamps and stands

▼ **Astronauts** have taken photographs of the Earth from space. These pictures show it is round.

A Cut out a strip of card. Label one end X and the other Y. Stick it down as shown. Put the boat at X. Put your eyes at the level shown. Pull the boat slowly with the string. Note which part of the boat you saw first. ▼

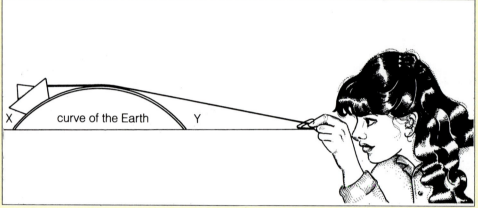

B Line up the torch and the two balls of plasticine as shown. When the Earth passes between the Sun and the Moon we can see its shadow on the Moon. Notice the shape of the shadow. ▶

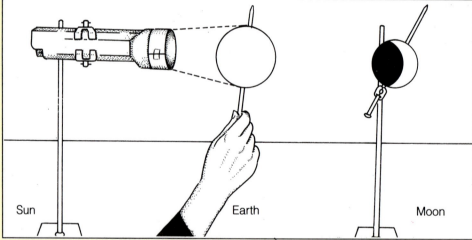

▼ The other planets in the Solar System are round. There is no reason why the Earth should be any different in shape to the other planets.

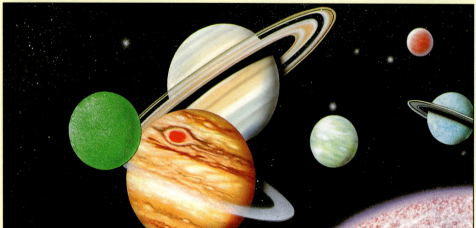

Q1 In **A** which part of the boat did you see first and which part did you see last?

Q2 How does **A** show that the Earth is round?

Q3 What is the shape of the Earth's shadow on the Moon?

Q4 Give two other reasons why we think the Earth is round.

2 The Earth

How the Earth moves

This experiment will help you understand how the Earth moves round the Sun.

Apparatus

☐ torch

A Work with a partner. The person acting as the *Sun* holds the torch and the person acting as the *Earth* stands two metres away in the light of the torch. ▼

B To show how the Earth turns about its own axis the person acting the Earth turns **anticlockwise** (to the left) on the same spot. ▼

C To show how the Earth moves round the Sun, *Earth* walks in an anticlockwise circle round the *Sun* but keeps turning anticlockwise as well. The *Sun* turns the torch slowly as the *Earth* moves round. ▼

D Complete one full turn around the *Sun*. In real time this would take **one year**, which is about 365 days (or to be more exact $365\frac{1}{4}$ days). Swap positions with your partner and repeat **A**, **B** and **C**. ▼

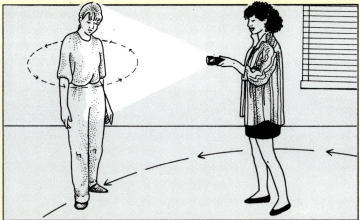

A leap year has 366 days in it

If we are very exact about the length of one year then we would say it is 365 days, 5 hours and 46 seconds. If we take the hours, minutes and seconds and multiply by four we get 23 hours, 15 minutes and 4 seconds. (This is almost one day.) Every fourth year the month of February has 29 days in it, instead of 28. Every fourth year is called a **leap year**.

Q1 Copy the diagram.

Q2 Put two arrows on your diagram to show how the Earth moves.

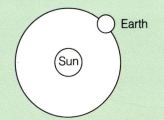

Q3 How many full turns does the Earth make about its own **axis**, when it travels once round the Sun?

Q4 How many months does it take the Earth to travel half-way round the Sun?

Q5 Which of the following years are leap years: 1976, 1982, 1988, 1990?

2 The Earth

Day and night

In this experiment you are going to learn why we have day and night. Our day is divided into 24 hours.

Apparatus
- globe of the Earth
- torch ☐ plasticine
- thin card ☐ sticky tape
- clamp and stand

A Make a small figure out of plasticine and place it on Britain. ▼

B In a darkened classroom shine the torch light on the figure as shown. When the figure is in the light it is day time. ▼

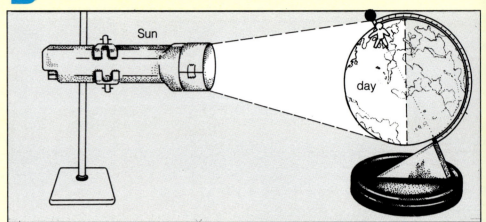

C Spin the globe slowly through half a turn anticlockwise. When the figure is in the dark it is night time. ▼

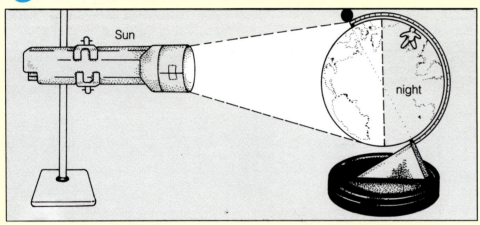

Day and night at the poles

▼ The **poles** have six months of days followed by six months of nights. When the North Pole is in the dark the South Pole is in the light. This is because the earth is spinning on a tilt.

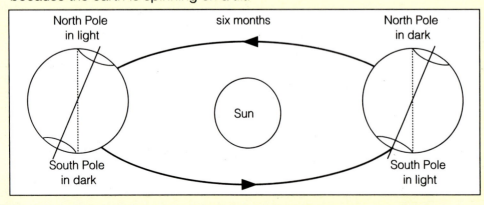

Q1 If you were at position X in the diagram below would it be day or night?

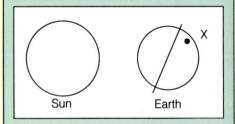

Q2 Why can only half of the Earth be in daylight at any one time?

Q3 Copy the diagram below:
a shade the *night* side
b label the *day* side
c draw and label the poles
d which pole is in the dark?

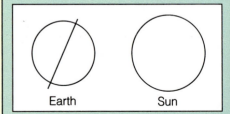

Q4 Explain why the poles have six months of light followed by six months of darkness.

2 The Earth

Earth facts

The Earth's tilt
▼ The imaginary line which the Earth spins about is called the Earth's axis. It is **tilted** by 23.5 degrees to the vertical.

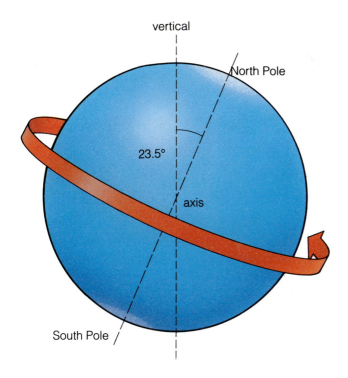

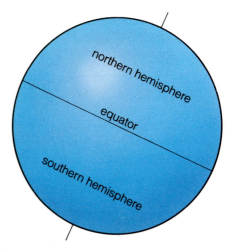

The equator
▲ The Earth is divided into two **hemispheres** (halves) by another imaginary line called the **equator**. There is the north half above the equator and the south half below the equator. For example, Britain and Europe are in the north half, and Australia and most of South America are in the southern hemisphere.

The direction of the Earth's axis
▼ The North and South Poles always point in the same direction no matter where the Earth is in its journey round the Sun.

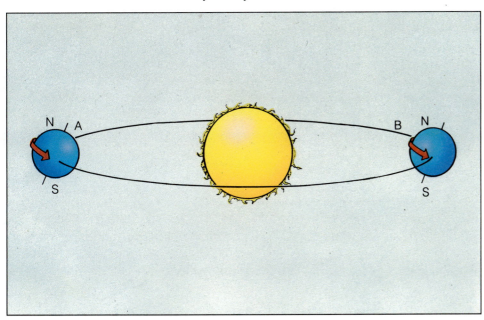

Q1 What is at each end of the Earth's axis?

Q2 Which line divides the Earth into two halves?
a What is the name of the top half?
b What is the name of the bottom half?
c Which half do we live in?

Q3 Look at the diagram on the left. Use the words **towards** and **away from** to copy and complete the following sentences.
a In position A the North Pole is tilted .... the Sun.
b In position B the North Pole is tilted .... the Sun.

2 The Earth

Sun's rays on the Earth

In this experiment you are going to see how the Earth's tilt affects the way the Earth is heated and the amount of daylight it receives.

Apparatus
- clamp and stand
- torch   globe

A Line up the globe and the torch, with the North Pole tilted away from the 'Sun' as shown. If possible darken the room. ▼

B Put the globe on the other side of the torch with the North Pole tilted towards the 'Sun' as shown. ▼

Winter and summer

▼ All through our winter less light and heat fall on the northern hemisphere because the Earth's axis is tilted away from the Sun. The Sun's rays have to travel further through the atmosphere and they also cover a greater area of land. Days are colder and dimmer.

▼ All through our summer more light and heat fall on the northern hemisphere, because the Earth's axis is tilted towards the Sun. The Sun's rays hit the Earth directly, they don't have to travel so far and they are spread over a smaller area of land. Days are hotter and brighter.

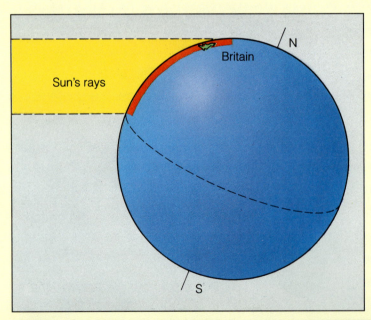

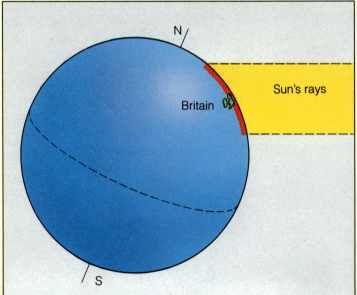

Q1 In **A** which half of the Earth got the most light?

Q2 In **B** which half of the Earth got the most light?

Q3 Which step shows the position of the Earth and Sun when we have our summer?

Q4 Draw a diagram to show the position of the Earth and the Sun when it is summer in the southern hemisphere.

2 The Earth

Seasons

This picture shows the Earth in four very important positions, as it **revolves** around the Sun. Each position is the beginning of a **season**. The labels refer to seasons in the northern hemisphere.

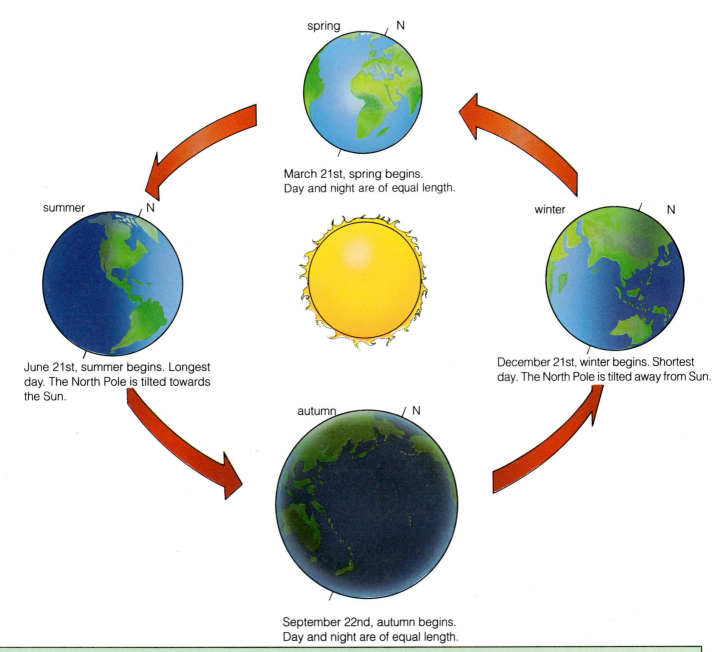

March 21st, spring begins. Day and night are of equal length.

June 21st, summer begins. Longest day. The North Pole is tilted towards the Sun.

December 21st, winter begins. Shortest day. The North Pole is tilted away from Sun.

September 22nd, autumn begins. Day and night are of equal length.

Q1 Draw a diagram of the Earth and the Sun to show the Earth's tilt during summer in the northern hemisphere.

Q2 What season is it in the southern hemisphere when the North Pole is pointing away from the Sun?

Q3 What would happen to the seasons if the Earth did not have a tilt?

Q4 Explain why it is that from December 21st to June 21st the day gets longer.

Q5 Imagine you lived at the North Pole – write a weather forecast to describe the amount of heat and light you would receive over 12 months.

3 Gravity

What on earth is gravity?

Gravity is the **force of attraction** between all pieces of **matter**.

▼ All things, large and small have gravity, but to feel the gravitational pull of something, it has to have a very large mass, for example like the Earth.

▼ Larger planets have a stronger pull of gravity than smaller planets.

▼ The force of gravity gets smaller as you move away from the Earth.

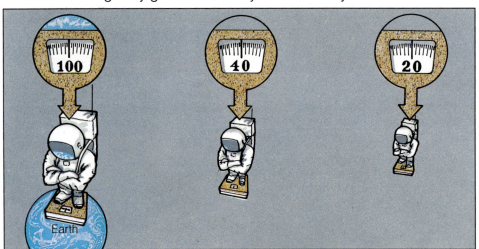

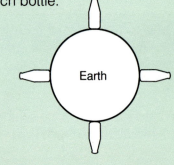

Since the day you were born you have been feeling the pull of the Earth's gravity on you. It's called your **weight**. Weight is another name for the force of attraction between your **mass** and the mass of the Earth. As you grow your mass gets bigger, so the force of attraction between you and the Earth gets bigger and this is why your weight gets bigger.

You have learnt that the Earth is shaped like a ball – it is gravity which stops us falling off it. It is the Sun's gravity which holds the planets in their circular paths around it. Gravity holds the Universe and all the things in it together.

Q1 What is gravity?

Q2 Why are astronauts lighter on the Moon than on the Earth, even though they have the same *mass*?

Q3 Jupiter's mass is almost 320 times the mass of the Earth. Which of these two planets has the largest pull of gravity?

Q4 Where would you have the greatest *weight*, on Jupiter or on the Earth?

Q5 The diagram below shows four bottles placed on the Earth's surface. Copy the diagram and draw what happens when a small amount of water is poured into each bottle.

3 Gravity

Measuring your mass and weight

In this experiment you are going to measure **your mass in kilograms** and convert it into **your weight in newtons**.

Apparatus

☐ bathroom scales ☐ calculator

Q1 Copy this table.

My mass (kg)	My weight (N)

weight = mass × gravitational pull
(N)   (kg)   (N/kg)

A Stand on the scales and record your mass in kilograms in the table. This is the amount of matter which you are made from. ▶

B Your weight depends on the pull of the planet you are standing on. Earth pulls down every kilogram at its surface with a force of 10 newtons (N). Use this equation to work out your weight and put it in the table. ▲

Q2 Copy this table.

Name of planet	Pull of gravity on the planet (N/kg)	My mass on the planet (kg)	My weight on the planet (N)
Mars	3.8		

Mars 3.8 N/kg

Saturn 11.9 N/kg

Jupiter 26.9 N/kg

Neptune 12.2 N/kg

C Look at the four pictures above. Each one shows a different planet and its **gravitational pull**. If you were standing on the surface of each planet calculate what your weight would be. Fill in your table. ▲

Q3 Where are you the lightest?

Q4 Where are you the heaviest?

Q5 Which measurement stays the same no matter which planet you are on?

3 Gravity

Living in zero gravity

In space the gravitational pull of planets and stars is very small because they are such a long distance away. Astronauts are therefore almost completely weightless.

▼ Astronauts can move with very little effort.

▼ Sleeping bags are fixed to the wall with straps so that astronauts cannot float around when sleeping.

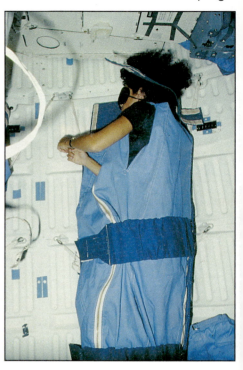

Living in space can have bad side-effects

▶ **Muscles** soon begin to weaken as they do not have to work against the pull of the Earth's gravity. Astronauts might be unable to walk when they return to Earth. A major problem is that the heart muscle also becomes smaller and weaker. To stop these things happening astronauts do a lot of **exercise** to keep their muscles strong. Exercise time can be as much as five hours a day. Any sweat produced must be vacuumed away to prevent water damage to the electronic equipment.

Another problem is that for the first two weeks in space astronauts have swollen faces and stuffy noses. This is because more blood goes from the legs to the head when there is no gravity.

Q1 What does zero gravity mean?

Q2 Can a mass have weight if there is no gravity?

Q3 Copy the diagram, and draw the path that each person's ball would take when it is thrown upwards.

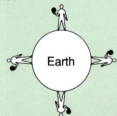

Q4 Why is there no *up* or *down* when there is no gravity?

Q5 Give two bad side-effects of zero gravity.

Q6 Give one advantage and one disadvantage of zero gravity.

Extension exercise 1 can be used now.

4 Spacecraft

The Space Shuttle

The Space Shuttle is the latest development in spacecraft design. This new generation spacecraft cuts the cost of space travel. Almost all of the Space Shuttle is reusable and this is what reduces the cost.

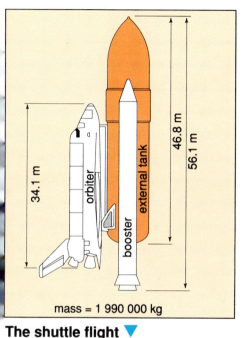

mass = 1 990 000 kg

◀ **Orbiter** (the space plane) is bolted on the back of a huge external fuel tank of liquid oxygen and hydrogen. Solid fuel booster rockets are also attached to the side of the tank to provide extra lift at take-off.

▶ All the fuel tanks are **jettisoned** (dropped off) when their fuel has been used. The plane is covered in heat resistant tiles to stop it burning up on re-entry. It can carry a 300 000 kilogram **payload** (for example a satellite or space station).

The shuttle flight ▼

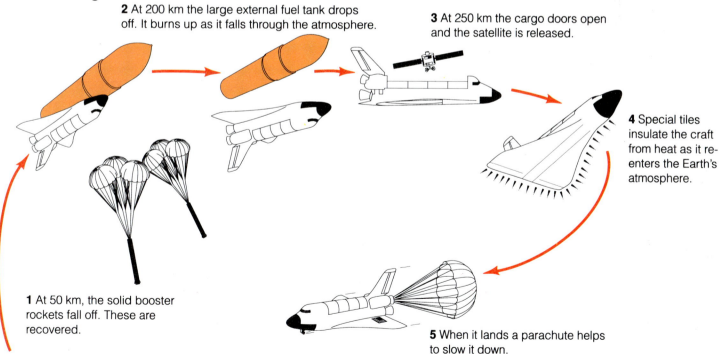

1 At 50 km, the solid booster rockets fall off. These are recovered.

2 At 200 km the large external fuel tank drops off. It burns up as it falls through the atmosphere.

3 At 250 km the cargo doors open and the satellite is released.

4 Special tiles insulate the craft from heat as it re-enters the Earth's atmosphere.

5 When it lands a parachute helps to slow it down.

Q1 What is the latest spacecraft design called?

Q2 Why is it less expensive than other rocket designs?

Q3 Name two things this spacecraft might take into space.

4 Spacecraft

Making a model Space Shuttle glider

Apparatus

☐ coloured felt-tip pens ☐ ruler
☐ paperclips ☐ sticky tape
☐ space plane cutout ☐ scalpel

⚠️ Take care when using the scalpel, it is very sharp.

In this activity you are going to make a model Space Shuttle glider and control its movement in the air.

A Cut the thick lines. *Score* the dotted lines. ▼

B The Space Shuttle is white but you can decorate your model in any colour you like. ▼

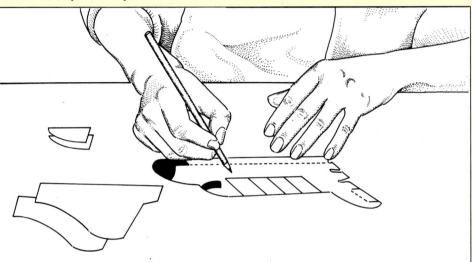

C Join the main wings to the **fuselage** by putting them in the slots. Strengthen the wings with tape above and below. Tape the front part of the wings in position. ▶

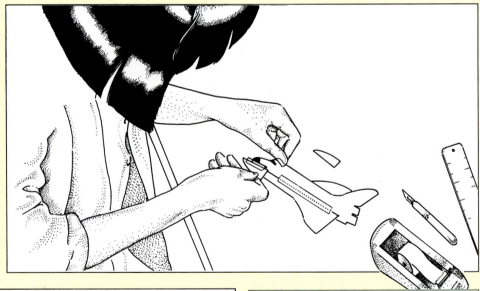

D Put some paper clips on the nose of the plane. Bend up the outer **elevons** (flaps at the back) to the angle shown below. See if you can bring the Space Shuttle down in a perfect glide. The landing should be soft and straight. ▼

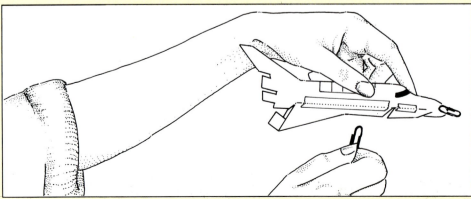

Q1 See if you can make the glider turn to the left and right by changing the elevon positions. Draw the elevon position for each turn.

Q2 See if you can make the glider *loop the loop*.
Draw the elevon position for this motion.

4 Spacecraft

Making your own rocket

In this experiment you are going to find out how rockets work.

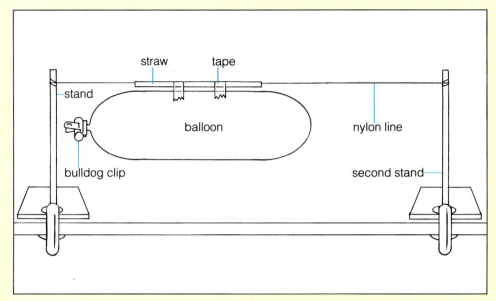

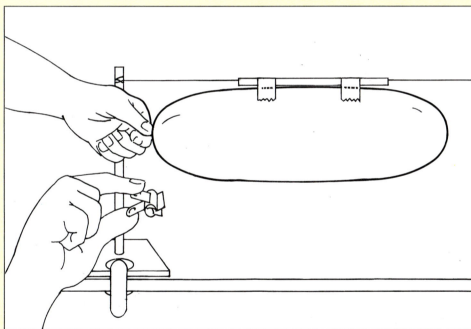

Apparatus

☐ straw ☐ bulldog clip
☐ nylon line ☐ sticky tape
☐ clamps and stands
☐ sausage-shaped balloon

A Blow up the balloon and seal the end with a bulldog clip. Arrange the balloon as shown. Tie each end of the nylon line to stands clamped to the bench. Make sure the line is pulled tight and that the balloon is free to slide. ◀

B Pinch the neck of the balloon with your fingers and remove the bulldog clip. Let the balloon go. ◀

Q1 What happened when you removed the bulldog clip and let go of the balloon?

Q2 Copy the drawing below. Add arrows to show the way the air goes and which way the balloon goes.

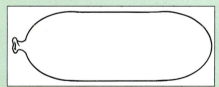

Q3 a Does a force act on the balloon?
b Give a reason for your answer.

Q4 Why do rockets need to be streamlined?

Rockets

There is no air in space, so propeller-driven aircraft cannot be used up there. Jet engines cannot be used either because they need **air** to burn the fuel which provides their **thrust**. Rockets carry a supply of **oxygen** in giant tanks. This oxygen is used to burn fuel which is then blasted out of the back of the rocket as a hot gas. The hot gas is pushed in one direction and the rocket is pushed in the other. Rockets need to be **streamlined** so that they can be pushed through the Earth's **atmosphere** more easily.

Extension exercise 2 can be used now.

4 Spacecraft

Satellites

A **satellite** is an object which orbits another larger one. The Moon is the Earth's **natural satellite**. Satellites which are launched into **orbit** around the Earth are called **artificial satellites**. They do not need to be streamlined (like rockets) because far above the Earth there is no air to be pushed through. Satellites use **solar panels** to change the Sun's rays into electricity for all their power needs. Satellites do many useful jobs.

Intelsat
▼ These are used to link people all over the world by telephone, television and computer.

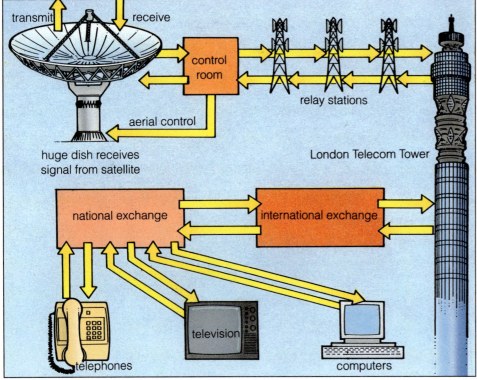

Landsat ▲
These help us to find gas and oil, keep track of pollution and give drought and famine warnings. Diseased crops show up blue-black and healthy crops in pink or red.

Teaching satellites
▼ These are television satellites. They are used to help people learn information in out-of-the-way places.

Sea satellites
▼ These are used to link signals from ships and oil rigs to the normal telephone network.

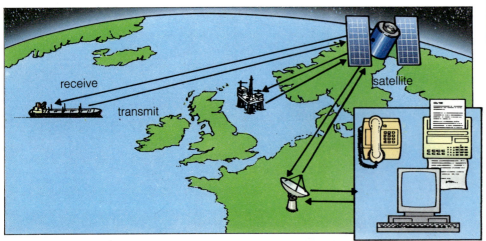

Q1 What is a satellite?

Q2 Why do satellites not need to be streamlined?

Q3 What are satellites used for?

Q4 What energy change takes place in the solar panels?

5 The Moon

How the Earth, Moon and Sun move

Apparatus
- [ ] scissors [ ] 3 paper fasteners
- [ ] Sun-Moon-Earth cutout

In this activity you are going to make a model to show how the Earth, Moon and Sun move.

A Cut round the circles on your sheet. Colour the *Sun* yellow, the *Earth* green and the *Moon* red. Use a paper fastener to join the two dots labelled S together. ▶

B Join together the three dots labelled E. Join the two dots labelled M together as in the picture. ▼

C You can show the movement of the Moon, Earth and Sun by turning the circles *anticlockwise*. ▼

Moon's orbit round the Earth

Earth's orbit round the Sun

Q1 Put arrows on your model to show how the Earth, Moon and Sun move.

Q2 Move the Earth through one turn. How long does it take the Earth to make one orbit of the Sun?

Q3 Move the Moon's disc through one turn. How long does it take the Moon to make one orbit of the Earth?

Q4 Start with the model you have made in the position below. Draw a diagram to show their position:
a 14 days later
b 6 months later.

Q5 In a group of 3, act out the motion of the Earth, Moon and Sun.

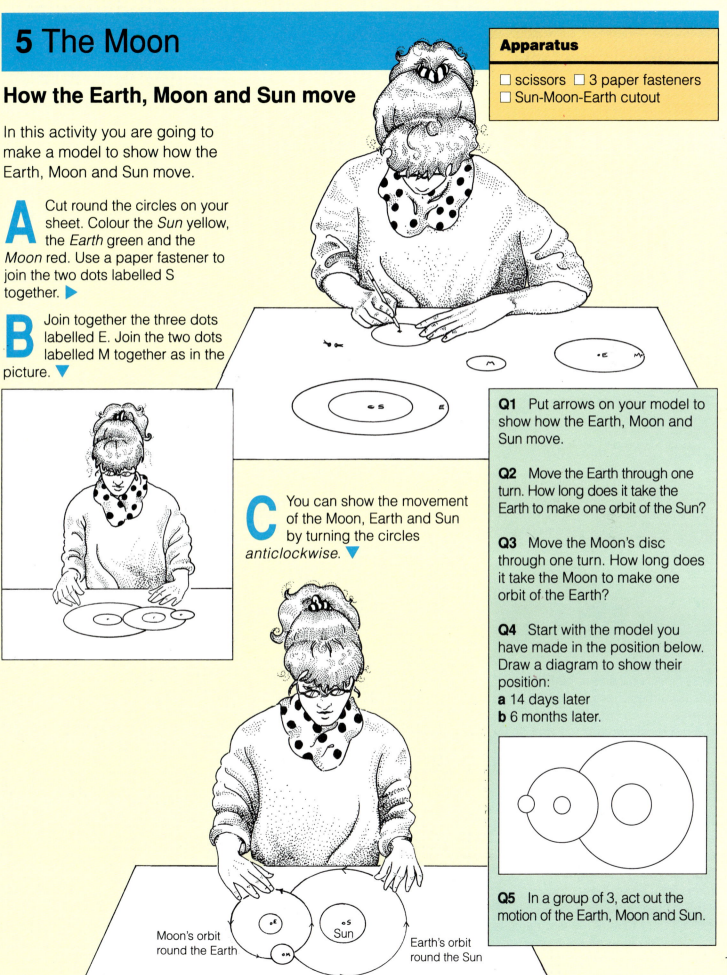

5 The Moon

The Moon – the facts

▼ The Moon is the Earth's closest neighbour in space. It is the brightest and closest object we see in the night sky yet it produces no light of its own. It looks bright because it **reflects** the Sun's rays.

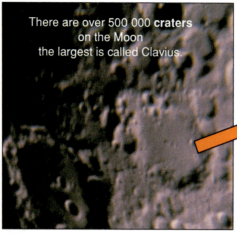

There are over 500 000 **craters** on the Moon the largest is called Clavius.

This shows the size of Clavius in relation to Britain.

▼ Gravity on the Moon is one sixth the pull of gravity on Earth. Astronauts can leap about with little effort.

▼ It would take 81 Moons to equal the mass of the Earth.

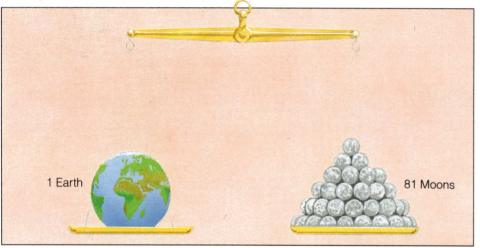

1 Earth   81 Moons

▶ There is no air on the Moon – it has no atmosphere, so there are no storms and no rain. Footprints left behind by astronauts will remain for millions of years. You cannot hear any sound because air is needed to carry sound from place to place.

Because there is no atmosphere to absorb the Sun's rays the daytime temperature on the Moon can be as high as 130 °C. At night the temperature can be as low as –153 °C because there is no atmosphere to slow down heat loss from the Moon's soil.

Q1 Why is the Moon so bright if it produces no light?

Q2 Why has the Moon got so many craters?

Q3 If you have a mass of 60 kg what weight would you be on the Moon? (Pull of gravity on Moon = 1.6 N/kg.)

Q4 Explain why not having an atmosphere can cause such large temperature differences between night and day.

5 The Moon

Phases of the Moon

When we look at the Moon it appears to change shape, from a very thin **crescent** to a full Moon and back again. The reason for this is that we see different amounts of the Moon's sunlit side as it goes around the Earth.

Apparatus
☐ big white ball or globe ☐ lamp ☐ pens ☐ paper

In the next experiment you are going to learn about the **phases** of the Moon and why they happen.

Q1 Copy this table.

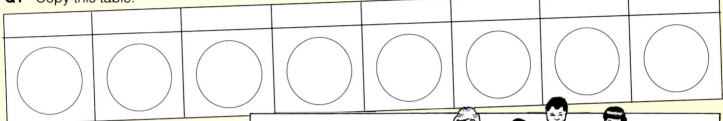

A Work in a group of nine. Put eight stools in a large circle and one in the centre. Place a lamp outside the centre as shown. The lamp represents the Sun. The person in the centre represents the Earth and the eight students on the stools represent the positions of the Moon as it circles the earth. The room should be darkened for this experiment. ▶

B Hold the ball in the light of the lamp and say what you think the view from the *Earth* is. Make a rough sketch. *Earth* tells you whether you are right or wrong and records her view accurately in her table. ▼

C When the ball has been around the full circle change positions and repeat the exercise a few times.

Q2 Complete the table for all positions of the Moon.

Q3 Look at these diagrams. For each diagram draw what the Moon would look like when seen from Earth.

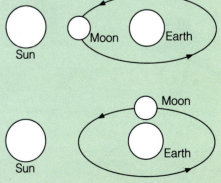

Extension exercise 3 can be used now.

5 The Moon

Project Moon base

Apparatus
- large sheets of paper
- felt-tip pens ☐ card ☐ plastic
- bottles ☐ wire ☐ straws
- glue ☐ aluminium foil
- Plasticine ☐ sand
- cardboard tubes

In ten years time the first bases on the Moon for people to live in may have been started. Earth is running short of important **metals** and **minerals** such as iron and aluminium, but there are huge amounts of them on the Moon and on other planets in our Solar System. Mining projects might be set up to **extract** (remove) the **ore** and send it back to Earth.

In this activity you are going to decide on the essential human needs of those who live in the Moon base. To do this imagine you are a Moon base astronaut.

A Work in a group. Make a list of the things the astronauts will need in the Moon base. ▼

B When you have finished, put the sheet where everyone else can see it. With your teacher's help produce one list of **essential** human needs. ▼

C Each group is to choose one or two human needs from the list. In your group think of ways in which the needs can be provided. Plan your ideas on a large sheet of paper. ▼

D Each group should select a representative to report back to the rest of the class, so that everyone can hear all the solutions. ▼

5 The Moon

E Use the materials provided to build models of your solutions. Finally put all the ideas together to make up one Moon Base. Display the Moon Base where your whole school can see it.

The picture below is an *artist's impression* of what a Moon base might look like. Advance planning is very important. Everything that goes into the Moon base has to be planned in detail, as forgetting something could cost you your life. ▼

Q1 Why do we need to build Moon bases?

Q2 List the important human needs the Moon base must provide for.

6 The planets

Planet sizes

Let us look at the other eight planets which orbit the Sun. They all move in the same direction as Earth and they travel in orbits which are almost circles. There are many differences between them.

In this activity you are going to make a scale model of the planets to see how they compare with the size of the Earth. ▼

Apparatus

☐ card ☐ ruler ☐ scissors
☐ drawing compasses
☐ Sun model

A The table shows a list of the planets (starting with the one nearest the Sun) and their sizes compared to the Earth. ▼

Planet	Relative size (cm)
Mercury	0.4
Venus	0.9
Earth	1.0
Mars	0.5
Jupiter	11.0
Saturn	9.4
Uranus	4.0
Neptune	3.8
Pluto	0.2

B Using the measurements in the table draw nine circles, one for each planet. Label each circle with the planet's name. Cut them out and put them in the same order as they are in the table. Put the Sun model next to Mercury. Compare the planet sizes. ▼

Q1 Copy this table.

Bigger than Earth	Smaller than Earth

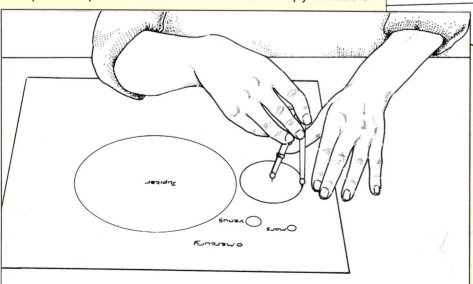

Q2 Fill in the table above with the names of the planets.

Q3 **a** How many planets are bigger than the Earth?
b How many planets are smaller than the Earth?

Q4 **a** Which is the largest planet?
b Which is the smallest planet?

Q5 How many Earths would fit across the diameter of the Sun?

6 The planets

How far away are the planets?

The distances between the planets are huge. Most of the Solar System is empty space. Travelling at just under 2 000 kilometres per hour it would take nearly 400 years to get to Pluto. The **outer planets** are cold and dark because they are furthest away from the Sun. The **inner planets** are very hot and get lots of sunlight because they are nearest the Sun.

In this activity you are going to compare how far away the planets are from the Sun.

Apparatus
☐ scale models of planets
☐ model of the Sun
☐ measuring tape

A Work in a group of ten. Choose a planet. This is the *planet* you are going to be in the activity. The table shows the average distances of the planets from the Sun. ▼

Planet	Average distance from Sun (million km)
Mercury	58
Venus	108
Earth	150
Mars	228
Jupiter	778
Saturn	1 427
Uranus	2 870
Neptune	4 497
Pluto	5 900

B Use a scale of 1 cm = **1Mkm**. (1Mkm = 1 000 000 km). Make a table with the names of the people in your group, the planet they are going to be and the distance they must stand from the Sun in centimetres. ▼

C Ask your teacher if you can carry out **B** outside or in a long corridor. The *Sun* should not move once the measurement begins. Measure your distance from the *Sun* and stay there until everyone has got into position. From your position look at the *Sun* and then at the other planets. Notice the scale of the distances. ▼

Q1 a Would the Sun look big or small from Mercury?
b Would it be hot or cold on Mercury?

Q2 Would the Sun look big or small from Neptune or Pluto?

Q3 Imagine you are on Pluto. Would the Sun look dim or bright?

Q4 Would it be cold or hot on Pluto?

Q5 Explain why it is colder and darker on the outer planets.

6 The planets

What's it like on the other planets?

Earth is the only planet known to support life. This is because it has water and oxygen and other things which support life. If it were closer to the Sun it would have been too hot for life to develop. If we were further away it would have been too cold. It was a delicate balance of **elements**, position and **temperature** which let living systems develop on Earth and not on the other planets.

Q1 Copy this table.

Name	Surface type	Average temperature	Type of atmosphere	Moons	Rings

Mercury
◀ Mercury has no atmosphere. It is rocky and covered in craters. It has an average temperature of 350 °C. It has no moons or rings. It has no life.

Venus
▼ Venus is covered with rocky craters and volcanic mountains. It has a thick atmosphere of **sulphuric acid** and **carbon dioxide** which stops heat loss. Its average temperature is 480 °C. It has no moons. It has no life.

Jupiter
▶ Jupiter has an atmosphere of **hydrogen**, **helium**, **ammonia** and **methane**. Its surface is all gas and its average temperature is –150 °C. It has 16 moons and one ring. There is no life on Jupiter.
▼ The **Red Spot** is a huge storm cloud. It is three times bigger than our Earth.

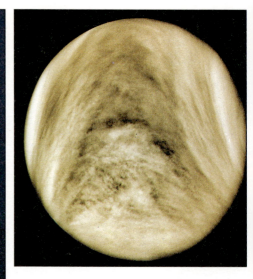

Io
Red Spot
Europa

Q2 Use the pictures and information above to fill in the table. Start with the planet nearest the Sun.

6 The planets

Saturn
▼ The surface is all gas – hydrogen, helium, ammonia and methane. The average temperature is –180 °C. It has at least 20 moons and many rings, but no life.

Mars
▼ It is rocky with lots of craters and volcanoes. The average temperature is –40 °C. The atmosphere is carbon dioxide. It has two moons and no life.

Neptune
▼ Its average surface temperature is –220 °C. It has two moons. Its surface is covered in gas made up of hydrogen, helium and methane. It has no life.

Saturn's rings
▼ The rings are made up of tiny rocky particles frozen in ice.

Pluto
▼ The surface is rocky. It is covered in solid frozen water and methane. Its average temperature is –230 °C. It has one moon and no rings. It has no life.

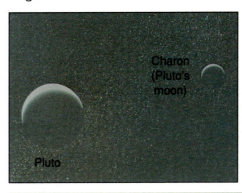

Uranus
▼ The surface is all gas – hydrogen, helium, ammonia and methane. It has five moons and 11 rings. The average temperature is –210 °C. It has no life.

Q3 Name the planets which have more than two moons.

Q4 Why do you think these planets have so many moons?

Q5 Which planets have no moons?

Q6 Why do you think these planets have no moons?

Q7 Why do you think Venus is hotter than Mercury even though Mercury is nearer the Sun?

Q8 Why do you think Pluto is frozen solid?

Q9 Explain why you think life developed on Earth and not on the other planets.

Extension exercise 4 can be used now.

7 Stars

The Sun is our nearest star

The Sun is an average size star. It is made up entirely of gas. The Sun is mostly made up of hydrogen gas. Due to the very large pressure and temperature at its centre, **nuclear fusion reactions** take place. Hydrogen gas is changed into helium gas and energy is given out in the process. This energy is **radiated** out to the Sun's surface (this is why it shines). The energy travels across space to the planets. We need this energy to live.

The nuclear reactions use up the hydrogen of the Sun. At least 4 million tonnes of matter is used up per second. It contains such a massive amount of gas however, that it will continue to burn for another 5 000 million years.

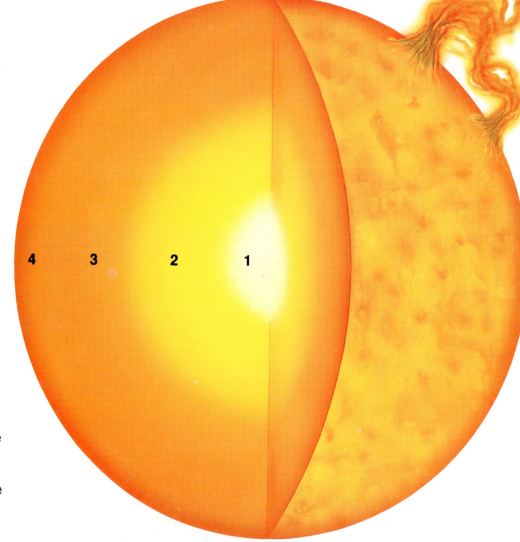

1 is the **core**. This is where the energy is produced by the nuclear reactions. The temperature is 15 million °C.
2 is the **radiative zone**. Energy travels outward in the form of radiation.
3 is the **convective zone**. Huge convection currents are just below the Sun's surface.
4 is the **photosphere**. This is the shiny bright surface of the Sun. The temperature is about 6000 °C.

Q1 Why is the Sun so important to the planet Earth?

Q2 Is the Sun a small star or a big star?

Q3 What is the temperature of **a** the centre **b** the surface?

Q4 Why is the Sun's mass getting less?

Q5 What do you think is happening to its pull of gravity?

7 Stars

Constellations

Throughout history people have seen patterns in the stars. The patterns are used to divide the sky up into groups of stars called **constellations**. There are 88 constellations altogether. **Astronomers** use the constellations to find their way around the night sky. Some famous ones are **Orion** (seen in winter), **Cygnus** (seen in summer) and the **Plough** and **Cassiopeia** (can be seen all year round). The stars are distant suns. Many may have their own planets. Stars look as if they are all at the same distance from Earth – but their distance away varies enormously. They also vary in size, temperature and colour.

This activity will help you find some of the constellations in the night sky.

Apparatus

☐ black paper ☐ tracing paper
☐ knitting needles and pins
☐ constellations hand-out
☐ pencil

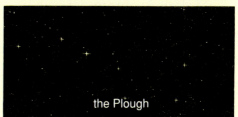
the Plough

A Trace each of the constellations from the hand-out onto black paper. Make big holes for bright stars and small holes for faint stars. ▶

B Place the constellation on an overhead projector in a darkened room. Turn it around so that you can recognise it from different directions. Test your friends. ▼

Q1 What is a group of stars called?

Q2 Name two famous groups of stars.

Q3 Why do you think some stars look big and bright and others look small and dim? (Try to give at least two reasons.)

Q4 Find at least 2 more constellations from a book and repeat **A** and **B**.

Extension exercise 5 can be used now.

7 Stars

The life of a star

▶ A large cloud of gas and dust (**nebula**) gathers together over millions of years. The gravity of the gas at the centre pulls the gas inward to form a huge gas ball. The cloud starts to get smaller and **denser**.

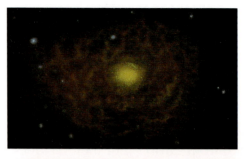

▶ Under the huge pressure the centre starts to break up into smaller bits. The bits are called **protostars** and they vary in size, from one tenth of a **light-year** to one light-year across. The protostars remain together inside the big black cloud in a **cluster**.

Type 1

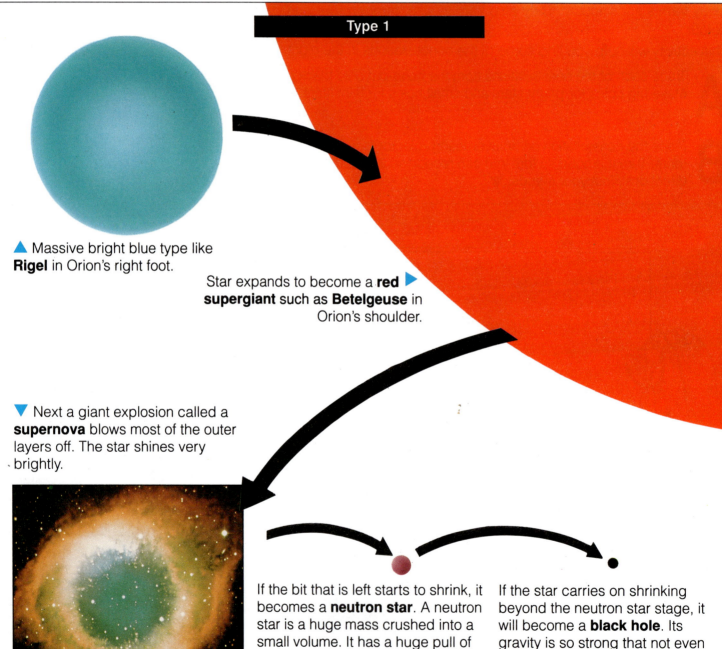

▲ Massive bright blue type like **Rigel** in Orion's right foot.

Star expands to become a **red supergiant** such as **Betelgeuse** in Orion's shoulder. ▶

▼ Next a giant explosion called a **supernova** blows most of the outer layers off. The star shines very brightly.

If the bit that is left starts to shrink, it becomes a **neutron star**. A neutron star is a huge mass crushed into a small volume. It has a huge pull of gravity. It spins very fast and sends out **radio waves**. For this reason, it is sometimes called a **pulsar**. ▲

If the star carries on shrinking beyond the neutron star stage, it will become a **black hole**. Its gravity is so strong that not even light can escape it. ▲

7 Stars

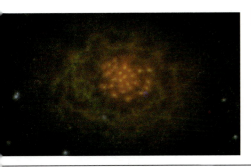

▶ Each protostar looks like a disc with a ball at the centre. The material in the disc could become the star's planets (its solar system). Depending on its mass the protostar can develop into one of two types of star.

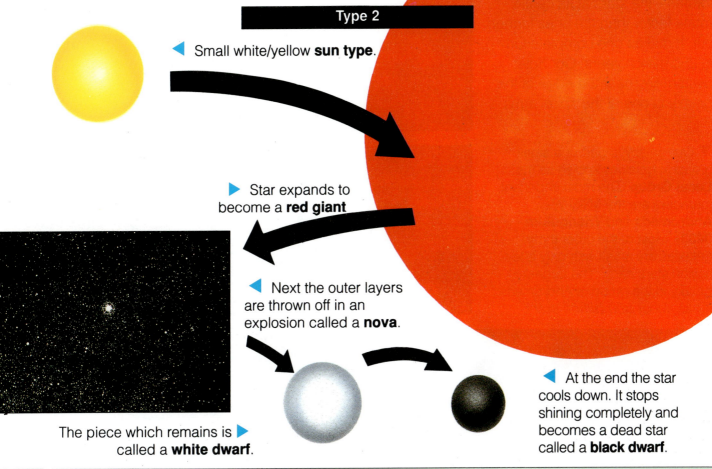

Type 2

◀ Small white/yellow **sun type**.

▶ Star expands to become a **red giant**

◀ Next the outer layers are thrown off in an explosion called a **nova**.

The piece which remains is ▶ called a **white dwarf**.

◀ At the end the star cools down. It stops shining completely and becomes a dead star called a **black dwarf**.

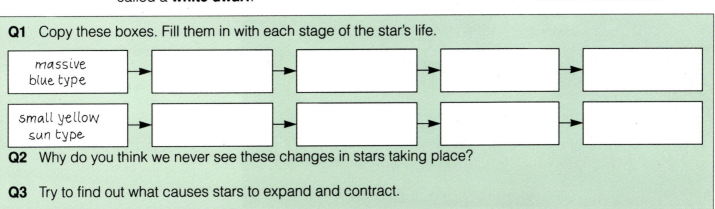

Q1 Copy these boxes. Fill them in with each stage of the star's life.

massive blue type	→		→		→		→	
small yellow sun type	→		→		→		→	

Q2 Why do you think we never see these changes in stars taking place?

Q3 Try to find out what causes stars to expand and contract.

Extension exercise 6 can be used now.

7 Stars

Galaxies

Our galaxy is called the Milky Way and our Sun is only one of its 100 billion stars. As well as stars our galaxy contains **nebulae** (dark and bright gas clouds), star clusters, and probably millions of planets too small and dark for us to see. The Milky Way also rotates – the stars at its centre rotate faster than the ones further out. It makes one complete turn in 250 million years. Our Solar System lies near the edge of the galaxy in one of the spiral arms.

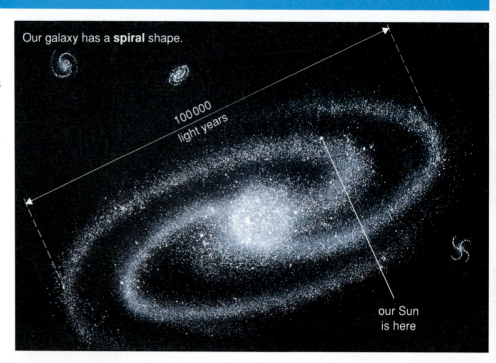

Our galaxy has a **spiral** shape.

100 000 light years

our Sun is here

▼ Our galaxy is part of a small group of galaxies known as the **Local Group**. The most important members are the Milky Way, **Andromeda** and **Triangulum (M33)**. Most of the other thirty galaxies are small with only a few million stars each. The largest galaxy in the group is Andromeda. It has about *300 billion stars*.

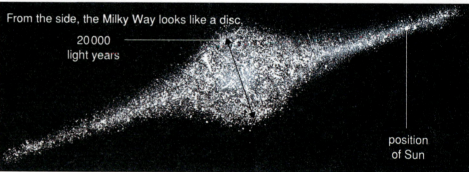

From the side, the Milky Way looks like a disc.

20 000 light years

position of Sun

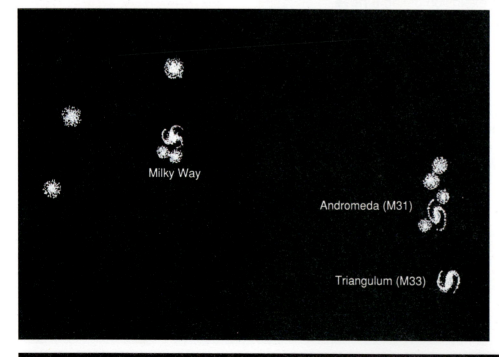

Milky Way

Andromeda (M31)

Triangulum (M33)

Q1 What is the name of our galaxy?

Q2 How many stars does our galaxy have in it?

Q3 Draw the shape of our galaxy.

Q4 Mark on your diagram the position of our Solar System.

Q5 Which is the biggest galaxy in the Local Group?

Q6 What difference would you notice if you looked towards the centre of the Milky Way and then looked towards the edge?

Extension exercise 7 can be used now.

7 Stars

The Universe

▼ The Universe contains everything that exists, the planets, their moons, the stars, star clusters, the galaxies and groups of galaxies and all the space and gas between them. As far as scientists know there is only one Universe and there is nothing which is not part of it.

The big bang
▲ Most scientists think that the Universe began with a massive explosion 15 000 million years ago. The explosion is called the **big bang**. All the matter which makes up the Universe was once together in a very small lump before the explosion took place.
Everything we see around us, (even our own bodies) was once part of the stars.

◀ Most galaxies are moving away from us. The whole of the Universe is **expanding** (spreading out). The galaxies got their **kinetic energy** (energy due to their movement) from the big bang explosion. There are millions of galaxies in the Universe.

> **Q1** What is the Universe?
>
> **Q2** What did the Universe look like before the big bang?
>
> **Q3** Where did the galaxies get their energy from to move apart?

Extension exercise 8 can be used now.

8 The future

Space stations and people living in space

The first factories are now being developed in space stations. There are electric **furnaces** on board both **Skylab** (USA) and **Salyut** (USSR) space stations. The furnaces could be used to produce metal to build further space stations from raw materials taken from the Moon. Flights from space stations to the Moon would cost much less than flights to and from Earth as Space Shuttles would not have to work against the strong pull of Earth's gravity or the resistance of the Earth's atmosphere.

Apparatus
- string ☐ ink ☐ water
- transparent plastic container
- pipette

In this activity you are going to act like a space station to see how it makes its own gravity. Look at the picture of a space station. ▼

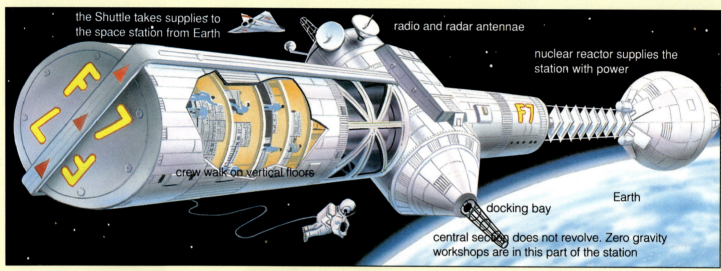

the Shuttle takes supplies to the space station from Earth

radio and radar antennae

nuclear reactor supplies the station with power

crew walk on vertical floors

docking bay

Earth

central section does not revolve. Zero gravity workshops are in this part of the station

A Put two holes in the plastic container and thread the string through. Add a little water and one drop of ink. ◀

B Gently start to spin the container. Raise your arm slowly until it is spinning horizontally. Notice what happens to the water. ▼

▼ Skylab did not rotate. Things floated weightlessly in it. This was because there was no force to hold things down. In rotating space stations astronauts can even have baths because the rotation **simulates** (acts like) gravity.

8 The future

Experiments in space
▶ Space is the ideal place for doing experiments. For example when gravity is almost zero there are no **convection currents** – liquids mix perfectly. Perfectly formed crystals can be grown. New medicines can be made. New alloys can be made as the metals mix perfectly.

Space travel
▼ Shuttles will make journeys into space as common as aeroplane flights. Space cities housing thousands of people will orbit the Earth. They will be built from materials mined from the Moon or the asteroids.

◀ Michelle Issel holds her Shuttle student experiment; it investigated crystal formation in weightlessness.

▼ Bean sprouts show unusual root growth in space.

Is there life out there?
▼ Scientists think that there could be as many as one million planets in our own galaxy which have life on them.

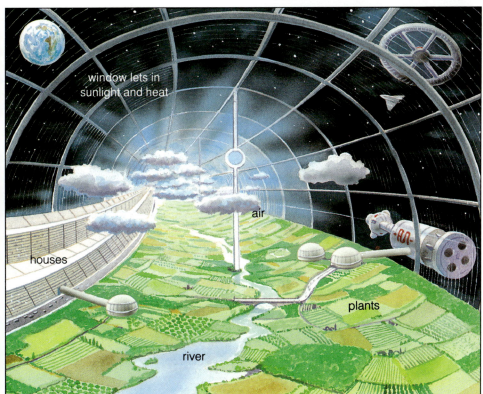

Q1 What happened to the water in **B**?

Q2 Draw a diagram to shown the position of the water in the container when it is spinning.

Q3 How does **B** help you to understand how gravity can be made on a space station?

Q4 Why is space an ideal place to do experiments?

Q5 Make a large drawing of your own space station and write a short report on what you think it would be like to live in it.

8 The future

For and against space exploration

1 Satellites give us better communication and weather forecasting.

2 Space research has made many useful discoveries.

3 If the large sums of money used for space research had been spent on cancer research, we might have found a cure by now.

4 Scientists should first solve real problems here on Earth rather than those in space projects.

5 Across the world, the space industry has provided employment for thousands of people.

6 Space probes have given us a lot of information about our Universe.

7 Exploring space has encouraged many different countries to work together on common projects.

8 Money should be spent to feed the starving millions in under-developed countries rather than on space exploration.

9 Space research could lead to the development of Star Wars weapons.

10 Human beings will not be happy just looking through telescopes – they are natural explorers.

11 Too many astronauts have lost their lives already in space disasters.

Q1 Copy this table.

Information number	For	Against	Reason

Q2 Read the information above. If you agree with it tick the *for* column, if you disagree tick *against*. Give a reason for your choice.

Q3 Think of at least two more reasons for or against space exploration.